Missouri Legal Research

CAROLINA ACADEMIC PRESS
LEGAL RESEARCH SERIES

Suzanne E. Rowe, Series Editor

ça.

Arizona, Second Edition—Tamara S. Herrera

Arkansas—Coleen M. Barger

California, Second Edition—Hether C. Macfarlane, Aimee Dudovitz
& Suzanne E. Rowe

Colorado—Robert Michael Linz

Connecticut—Jessica G. Hynes

Federal, Second Edition—Mary Garvey Algero, Spencer L. Simons,
Suzanne E. Rowe, Scott Childs & Sarah E. Ricks

Florida, Fourth Edition—Barbara J. Busharis, Jennifer LaVia
& Suzanne E. Rowe

Georgia—Nancy P. Johnson, Elizabeth G. Adelman & Nancy J. Adams

Idaho, Second Edition—Tenielle Fordyce-Ruff & Kristina Running

Illinois, Second Edition—Mark E. Wojcik

Iowa—John D. Edwards, M. Sara Lowe, Karen L. Wallace
& Melissa H. Weresh

Kansas—Joseph A. Custer & Christopher L. Steadham

Kentucky—William A. Hilyerd, Kurt X. Metzmeier & David J. Ensign

Louisiana, Second Edition—Mary Garvey Algero

Massachusetts—E. Joan Blum

Michigan, Second Edition—Pamela Lysaght & Cristina D. Lockwood

Minnesota—Suzanne Thorpe

Mississippi—Kristy L. Gilliland

Missouri, Third Edition—Wanda M. Temm & Julie M. Cheslik

New York, Third Edition—Elizabeth G. Adelman, Theodora Belniak,
Courtney L. Selby & Brian Detweiler

North Carolina, Second Edition—Scott Childs & Sara Sampson

Ohio, Second Edition—Sara Sampson, Katherine L. Hall & Carolyn Broering-Jacobs

Oklahoma—Darin K. Fox, Darla W. Jackson & Courtney L. Selby

Oregon, Third Edition—Suzanne E. Rowe

Pennsylvania—Barbara J. Busharis & Bonny L. Tavares

Tennessee—Sibyl Marshall & Carol McCrehan Parker

Texas, Revised Printing—Spencer L. Simons

Washington, Second Edition—Julie Heintz-Cho, Tom Cobb
& Mary A. Hotchkiss

West Virginia—Hollee Schwartz Temple

Wisconsin—Patricia Cervenka & Leslie Behroozi

Wyoming—Debora A. Person & Tawnya K. Plumb

ça.

Missouri Legal Research

Third Edition

Wanda M. Temm

Julie M. Cheslik

Suzanne E. Rowe, Series Editor

CAROLINA ACADEMIC PRESS

Durham, North Carolina

Library of Congress Cataloging-in-Publication Data

Temm, Wanda M., author.
  Missouri legal research / Wanda M. Temm and Julie M. Cheslik. --
Third edition.
      pages cm. -- (Legal Research Series)
  Includes bibliographical references and index.
  ISBN 978-1-61163-711-3 (alk. paper)
  1. Legal research--Missouri. 2. Law--Missouri. I. Cheslik, Julie M.,
author. II. Title.

  KFM7875.T46 2015
  340.072'0778--dc23

                              2015018518

Carolina Academic Press
700 Kent Street
Durham, North Carolina 27701
Telephone (919) 489-7486
Fax (919) 493-5668
www.cap-press.com

Printed in the United States of America.

For Keith and Bettie Sue Shumway,
whose passion for higher education
instilled in me the drive
to be the best teacher I can be.

— WMT

For Marlene L. Cheslik,
My Teacher.

— JMC

Summary of Contents

Contents

List of Tables and Figures

Tables

Figures

Series Note

The Legal Research Series published by Carolina Academic Press includes titles from states around the country as well as a separate text on federal legal research. The goal of each book is to provide law students, practitioners, paralegals, college students, laypeople, and librarians with the essential elements of legal research in each jurisdiction. Unlike more bibliographic texts, the Legal Research Series books seek to explain concisely both the sources of state law research and the process for conducting legal research effectively.

Foreword

Judge Laura Denvir Stith
Supreme Court of Missouri

The substantive classes that a law student takes teach the fundamental principles, concepts, and rules underlying particular areas of law. The knowledge gained in these classes will prove invaluable to the practicing lawyer. But, an understanding of how to undertake effective legal research is essential to being a successful law student and, more importantly, to becoming an effective lawyer. If one does not know what a regulation is, or how to find out whether a case is still good law, then the substantive knowledge gained in law school will be of little practical use to the student or a future client. The gap between acquiring substantive knowledge and providing helpful advice is filled by legal research.

Students of Professors Wanda Temm and Julie Cheslik at the University of Missouri-Kansas City have long had the benefit of their insights into legal research methods. I am delighted that they have chosen to publish their ideas so that others will have the opportunity to gain from their experience. *Missouri Legal Research* offers a clear guide to the various sources of law used by Missouri lawyers and gives insights into how to make legal research both useful and effective. There are so many ways to approach legal research, and so many research sources to choose from, that a new student often is not sure where to begin. This book carefully explains the different types of sources of law, which sources are best used for what purpose, and how to quickly find relevant laws or cases.

Missouri Legal Research shows how to find cases that apply the relevant concepts, how to research statutes and regulations that set out the governing rules, and how to use treatises and law reviews to explain to a dubious judge or senior partner why the principles embodied in those cases should apply to the case at hand. In short, it teaches the skills the new law student needs in order to solve the mysteries of legal research.

Further, *Missouri Legal Research* has the added advantage of offering this excellent primer on legal research in a context that will be specifically useful to students in Missouri law schools who wish to become Missouri lawyers. Professors Temm and Cheslik explain the structure of the Missouri court system and the judicial decision-making process, thereby providing a useful context for understanding how and why particular types of research are useful and necessary. This book's suggestions are practical, and are geared to Missouri law and to the peculiarities of Missouri practice.

I am confident that this book will be a ready reference to all who find their way to its pages. Students will refer to this book time and again while taking legal research and writing, in preparing moot court briefs, and as they research issues for seminar papers or for legal clinics. New lawyers will find it invaluable when their work requires research into sources they have not utilized since their first-year courses. *Missouri Legal Research* is an invaluable addition to Missouri's law libraries.

Preface and Acknowledgments

This book is intended primarily for use by the student who is new to legal research or an area of legal research. Other audiences include practitioners who need to be familiar with Missouri resources, as well as paralegals, college students, and laypeople. While some chapters may serve a reference-type purpose, such as the legislative history chapter, this book is primarily intended as an introduction to the tools and sources of Missouri and federal legal research. Excerpts of sample pages are included to help orient readers to the various resources. The format of sample pages may be altered to fit this book's smaller page size.

Structure and Themes

Each chapter of this book introduces one type of authority or a finding tool. The focus of each chapter is on a tripartite process: (1) At what stage of legal problem-solving is this source helpful? (2) How do legal researchers access and use this source? (3) How is this source updated?

In addition to the three process-oriented queries, there are four common themes to remember in learning about the sources of legal research. These themes consider whether a source is (1) primary vs. secondary authority, (2) mandatory vs. persuasive authority, (3) official vs. unofficial, and (4) compiled chronologically vs. topically. These themes will be addressed frequently throughout the book.

Print and Online Sources

This book focuses on the sources of law (statutes, case law, rules, regulations, etc.) both in a print medium and in an online format. After explaining the print sources and how they are compiled and used to solve legal problems, each chapter shows how researchers can access these sources in an online format. An important aspect of the book is its discussions of how to make judgments about which medium to access and when to access it.

Online sources are divided into free-access Internet sites and fee-based online databases. Unlike print resources that make format changes on an infrequent basis, online sources change format and content much more often. As a result, changes can occur online before a research book that describes that online source has left the printer. Indeed, the two major fee-based online databases, WestlawNext and Lexis Advance, issue new format changes on an almost annual basis.

Reflection

This book began as *The UMKC Legal Research Guide* in 1994, originally drafted by Julie Cheslik. Since then it has been updated annually. In 1999, Wanda Temm took the reins as Director of Legal Writing and continued the annual update. Over the years, the guide evolved to become a resource for students well after the first year of law school. Numerous alumni maintained their copies and used the guide in their practices and clerkships. Through their suggestions that it be made available to a wider audience, this book was written.

Acknowledgments

This book is the work of many people, primarily former teaching assistants in the Legal Writing Program at the University of Missouri-Kansas City School of Law, who contributed early outlines, early chapter drafts, examples, and, above all, enthusiasm and dedication. Particular thanks to former teaching assistants Teresa Locke, Mark Dover, Tony Gosserand, Dianne Hansen, Barbara Hircock, Robert James, Elizabeth Lawrence, Derrick Pearce, Jacque Sparks, Roger Walker, Steve Ward, and Louie Wright, who helped start this project.

Many thanks to our current and former legal writing colleagues, Barbara Wilson, Judith Popper, Aaron House, Marcia Cook, and Shirley Goza, and administrative assistants, Norma Karn, Elizabeth Couzens, and Jackie Capranica, who have seen this manuscript in its various forms too many times. Their support has been unending and their contributions too numerous for words.

Special thanks to Lawrence MacLachlan, Director of Research and Instructional Services, Leon E. Bloch Law Library, University of Missouri-Kansas City School of Law, for his patient and consistent review. He added valuable explanations and illustrations based on his years of experience teaching legal research. Thanks also to Rachelle Leutzinger for her assistance on the graphical information and to Pam Benton for her contributions to the Missouri legislative history section.

Series editor, Suzanne Rowe, also deserves special thanks. In addition to contributing portions of Chapter 1 and Appendix A, her able assistance in finalizing the manuscript and suggesting improvements has helped make this book even more readable and user-friendly. Her dedication to this project was invaluable.

Thanks as well to Dean Ellen Suni, the UMKC administration, and the UMKC law faculty for their support of the Legal Writing Program over the years. That support has allowed us to provide our students a top-notch program using innovative teaching methods. This book would not have been created without their support.

WMT and JMC

Missouri Legal Research

Chapter 1

The Legal Research Process

I. Legal Research Generally

The fundamentals of legal research are the same in every American jurisdiction, though the details vary. While some variations are minor, others require specialized knowledge of the resources available and the analytical framework in which those resources are used. This book introduces the legal research resources, processes, and analysis required to be a thorough and effective legal researcher.[1] While this book focuses on Missouri law, it supplements this focus with explanations of research into federal law and the law of other states, both to introduce additional resources and to highlight some of their variations.

This book is not designed to be a blueprint of every resource in the law library or search engine on the Internet; many resources contain their own detailed explanations in a preface or a "Help" section. This book is more like a manual or field guide, introducing the resources needed at each step of the research process and explaining how to use them.

---

1. For lawyers, conducting thorough and proper legal research is not only an important part of an attorney's role in assisting clients—it is a professional obligation. The Missouri Rules of Professional Conduct cover all aspects of legal practice. See Rules of Professional Conduct at www.mobar.org or on the Missouri Judiciary's website at www.courts.mo.gov/page.jsp?id=707. One part of the Rules states: "A lawyer shall provide competent representation to a client. Competent representation requires the legal knowledge, skill, thoroughness and preparation reasonably necessary for the representation." Disciplinary Rule 4-1.1. A large part of this knowledge and preparation comes from legal research. This book provides instruction in how to conduct effective and efficient research into Missouri law.

3

II. The Intersection of Legal Research and Legal Analysis

One cannot perform legal research without using legal analysis. The skills are intertwined. Legal analysis is interwoven throughout the legal research process. In researching the law, whether using print resources or online sources, you have to decide which words to search and which index entry or online database looks most promising. Moreover, when you read the text of a document, you will need legal analysis skills to determine whether it is truly relevant to your client's situation. You will also use analytical skills to decide whether one resource is more applicable to your client's circumstances than another. This intersection of research and analysis makes legal research difficult, especially for the novice. While this book's focus is legal research, it also discusses the fundamental aspects of legal analysis that are required to conduct research competently.

III. Overview of the Legal Research Process

The goal of legal research is to locate legal authority that resolves an issue, problem, or dispute. Many different types of legal authority may resolve or help to resolve a legal problem. Legal authority includes the law itself in the form of constitutions, statutes, case law, and administrative rules or regulations. Legal authority also includes sources that are not the law, such as articles by scholars who advocate what the law should be in a given situation.

All legal authority can be categorized into two types: primary authority or secondary authority. *Primary authority* is the law itself, enacted, pronounced, or adopted by an entity with law-making power. Primary authority includes constitutions and statutes enacted by legislative bodies, case law pronounced by courts, and rules and regulations adopted by administrative agencies, as well as adjudicative decisions of administrative agencies. *Secondary authority* includes all other legal sources, such as treatises, law review articles, and legal encyclopedias. While secondary authorities are not the law, they can aid you in understanding the law and in locating primary authority.

In addition to being categorized as either primary or secondary, legal authority is also classified as either mandatory or persuasive. *Mandatory authority*, also called *binding authority*, is legal authority that is binding on the

Table 1-1. Examples of Authority in Missouri Research

	Mandatory Authority	Persuasive Authority
Primary Authority	Missouri statutes Missouri Supreme Court cases Missouri regulations	Illinois statutes Kansas Supreme Court cases Arkansas regulations
Secondary Authority	——	Law review articles Legal encyclopedias Treatises

decision-maker in resolving a legal issue, problem, or dispute. For example, on a legal question involving Missouri state law, mandatory or binding authority includes the Missouri Constitution, statutes enacted by the Missouri legislature, opinions of the Supreme Court of Missouri,[2] and Missouri administrative regulations.

Persuasive authority is not binding but may be followed by the decision-maker if it is relevant and well-reasoned. Authority is merely persuasive, as opposed to binding, if it is (1) from a different jurisdiction or (2) not produced by an entity with law-making power. On a question of Missouri law, examples of persuasive authority include a similar statute from another state, an opinion of a state court in another jurisdiction, and a law review article. Notice in Table 1-1 that persuasive authority may be either primary or secondary authority, while mandatory authority is always primary. Stated another way, secondary authority can never be mandatory or binding because secondary authority is not the law—it is not produced by an entity with the power to make law.

The goal or focus of legal research is to locate primary, mandatory authority. Within primary, mandatory authority, there is an interlocking hierarchy of constitutions, statutes, case law, and administrative regulations. A jurisdiction's constitution is the supreme law of that jurisdiction. If a statute is on point, that statute comes next in the hierarchy, followed by administrative rules. Judicial opinions may interpret the statute or rule, but they cannot disregard either. A judicial opinion may, however, decide that a statute violates the constitution or that a rule oversteps its bounds. If no constitutional provision,

---

2. Missouri trial courts must follow an opinion of the Missouri Court of Appeals if the Supreme Court of Missouri has not addressed the issue.

statute, or administrative rule is on point, the issue will be controlled by the *common law* or judge-made law.

IV. Approaches to Research

Because the goal of legal research is to locate legal authority (ideally primary, mandatory authority) that resolves or helps resolve an issue, dispute, or problem, it is helpful to have a systematic process for locating that authority. Three approaches to legal research can be used with virtually every legal research resource, both online and in print.

(1) The Known-Authority Approach[3]

(2) The Known-Topic Approach[4]

(3) The "Know-Nothing" or Descriptive-Word Approach

This chapter briefly describes each of these approaches and when to use them. Subsequent chapters explore how to use each of the three approaches with specific types of legal resources.

The *known-authority approach* is used when the legal researcher knows about a specific legal authority that resolves or might resolve the issue. For example, the researcher might have the name of or even a citation to a case that may resolve the issue. When you possess that type of a head start, it is almost always best to start by locating, reading, and analyzing the known authority. Even if the known authority is not dispositive, it will often lead to other authorities that are more relevant.

The *known-topic approach* is typically used when the researcher already has a general understanding of the area of law and can determine the general legal issue based on that knowledge. This approach is most often used successfully by legal researchers who have some experience with a wide variety of legal topics and know how those topics might be labeled or named in legal resources. For example, in researching the rights and duties of parties to a residential real estate contract, an experienced legal researcher in that area of the law might know that the parties to such a contract are often referred to as "vendor" and "purchaser." A researcher without that experience would not know to incorporate those terms into her search.

---

3. Christopher G. Wren & Jill Robinson Wren, *The Legal Research Manual* 45 (2d ed. 1986).

4. *Id.*

Beginning legal researchers almost invariably benefit from implementing the *know-nothing* or *descriptive-word approach* to legal research. This approach is used when the researcher is unfamiliar with the specifics of an area of law or simply does not know where to begin researching a legal issue. This approach is called the descriptive-word approach because it involves generating a list of research terms to describe the legal issue, problem, or dispute. These terms are then looked up in the index of a print legal resource or used to search an online database.

A. Generating Descriptive Words

Many legal resources in print intend their lengthy indexes to be the starting point for finding legal authority. Electronic sources often require the researcher to enter words that are likely to appear in the synopsis or full text of relevant documents. To ensure that you are thorough in beginning a research project, you will create a comprehensive list of words, terms, and phrases that may lead to law on point. These may be legal terms or common words that describe the client's situation. The items on this list are called *descriptive words*.

Organized brainstorming is the best way to compile a comprehensive list of descriptive words. Some researchers generate their descriptive words by asking the journalistic questions: Who? What? Where? When? Why? and How? Other researchers use a mnemonic device like TARPP, which stands for Things, Actions, Remedies, People, and Places,[5] to generate a list of descriptive words. Whether you use one of these suggestions or develop your own method, your goal is the same: to generate a broad range of descriptive words regarding the facts, issues, and desired solutions of your client's situation. Include in the list both specific and general words to maximize the chances of finding relevant authority. Try to think of synonyms and antonyms for each term since at this point you are uncertain which terms an index may include. A legal dictionary or thesaurus may help to generate additional terms. Remember not to focus your research terms exclusively on the facts of your case—be sure to address desired solutions and legal issues.

As an example, assume you are working for a defense attorney who was recently assigned to a burglary case. Around midnight, your client allegedly bent a credit card to spring the lock to a stereo store, where she stole $2,000 worth

---

5. *See* Steven M. Barkan et al., *Fundamentals of Legal Research* 15 (10th ed. 2015) (explaining "TARP," a similar mnemonic device).

Table 1-2. Generating Descriptive Words

Journalistic Approach

Who:	Thief, robber, burglar, business owner, property owner
What:	Burglary, possession, second degree, crime
Where:	Store, building, commercial establishment, business, shop
When:	Midnight
Why:	Theft, stealing, stolen goods
How:	Breaking and entering, burglar tools, trespassing

TARPP Approach

Things:	Burglar tools, stolen goods
Actions:	Burglary, possession, breaking and entering, trespassing, damages, crime
Remedies:	First degree, second degree, incarceration
People:	Thief, robber, burglar, business owner, property owner
Places:	Store, building, commercial establishment, business, shop

of equipment. She was charged with second-degree burglary and possession of burglar tools. You have been asked to determine whether a good argument exists that she cannot be guilty of the possession charge based on her use of a credit card rather than professional burglar tools. Table 1-2 provides examples of descriptive words you might use to begin this research project.

As your research progresses, you will learn new descriptive words to include in your list and decide to take others off. For example, you may find keywords that judges tend to use in discussing your topic. Or you may learn a *term of art*: a word or phrase that has special meaning in a particular area of law. These terms need to be added to the list and may even provide a shortcut to the known-topic approach.

B. Researching the Law — Organization of This Text

The remainder of this book explains how to use your descriptive words to conduct legal research in a variety of sources. Although the research process often begins with secondary sources, this book begins with primary authority because finding that authority is the goal of legal research. Each chapter explains how to use both print and online sources to locate authority.

Chapter 2 addresses enacted law including the Missouri Constitution, which is the highest legal authority in the state, and statutes, which are laws passed by the legislature. Chapter 3 explains how to use case reporters and digests to research judicial decisions. Chapter 4 addresses administrative law and is the last of the chapters that focus on primary authority. The chapters that follow explain how to update legal authority using citators (Chapter 5), how to use secondary sources and practice aids (Chapter 6), and how to research legislative history to help interpret legislative intent (Chapter 7). Although each chapter explains how to use the known-authority approach and known-topic approach to legal research in online sources as well as including relevant website addresses for online research, Chapter 8 delves into the advantages and disadvantages of online research and provides basic information for conducting legal research online using descriptive words. Chapter 9 discusses research strategies, how to organize your research, and when to stop.

Appendix A provides an overview of the conventions lawyers follow in citing legal authority in their documents. Appendix B contains a selected bibliography of texts on legal research and analysis. The general research texts tend to concentrate on federal resources, supplementing this book's introduction to those resources.

Chapter 2

Constitutions and Statutes

This chapter introduces two types of primary authority—constitutions and statutes. Constitutions are the fundamental law of a nation or state. They establish the form of government and delegate governmental functions to different departments. Statutes are laws created and enacted by the legislative branch of government.

I. Constitutions

A. Missouri Constitution

1. History and Scope

"We, the people of Missouri, with profound reverence for the Supreme Ruler of the Universe, and grateful for His goodness, do establish this constitution for the better government of the state."[1]

Missouri's first state constitution was adopted by convention on July 19, 1820, and Missouri was admitted to the Union on August 10, 1821. Revisions were made to the constitution in 1865. The 1865 constitution, sometimes referred to as the "Drake Constitution," was developed in the aftermath of the Civil War. Written by anti-slavery proponents, the revised constitution included provisions requiring a loyalty oath and restricting voting rights to Union loyalists. After a change in political control, the constitution was again revised in 1875. This third constitution was extremely detailed and included restrictions on legislative powers.

Missouri voters adopted a fourth revised constitution in 1945 after approval by a majority of delegates at the Constitutional Convention.[2]

---

1. Mo. Const. preamble.
2. Debates, journals, and proceedings for the various constitutional conventions

The provisions of the Missouri Constitution parallel many of the most familiar provisions of the United States Constitution. Article I of Missouri's constitution ensures religious freedom, freedom of speech, and the right to peaceable assembly. Articles II through V provide for the legislative, executive, and judicial departments of the state government.

Unlike the U.S. Constitution, the Missouri Constitution is frequently amended. Under Article XII, the Missouri Constitution may be amended by the voters. Proposed amendments are placed on the ballot by the General Assembly or by initiative.[3] Amendments have ranged along the political scale. For example, the "Hancock Amendment" requires voter approval before taxes are imposed above a defined limit.[4] In the 2006 election, Missouri voters approved an amendment that allows stem cell research as permitted under federal law.[5] The Missouri Constitution provides that the General Assembly or the Secretary of State may submit to the voters every twenty years the question of whether a convention should be called to revise or amend the constitution.[6]

Like many state constitutions, the Missouri Constitution also covers some issues often thought of as being statutory in nature. For example, Article III, Section 39(a) authorizes the game of bingo by religious, charitable, fraternal, veteran, or service organizations. Figure 2-1 lists the articles of Missouri's constitution. Because of the breadth of issues covered, you should check to see whether a constitutional provision affects your research problem even when that possibility may seem unlikely.

2. Researching the Missouri Constitution

The Missouri Constitution is published as part of *Revised Statutes of Missouri* (RSMo),[7] currently in volume 20. An index specifically for the constitution follows the constitution's printed text. References to the constitution are included in the General Index. The Missouri Constitution is also published as part of *Vernon's Annotated Missouri Statutes* (VAMS).

---

are available in the Missouri Secretary of State's Archives at www.sos.mo.gov/archives/ history and through the MERLIN search engine of the University of Missouri system's library catalogs.

3. Mo. Const. art. XII, § 2(b).

4. Mo. Const. art. X, § 18(3).

5. Mo. Const. art. III, § 38(d).

6. Mo. Const. art. XII, § 3(a).

7. The title page of the official code is entitled *Revised Statutes of the State of Missouri*. The spine indicates the title as *Missouri Revised Statutes*. This book will refer to the official code as *Revised Statutes of Missouri* or RSMo.

Figure 2-1. Missouri Constitution Table of Contents

		PREAMBLE
ARTICLE	I	BILL OF RIGHTS
	II	THE DISTRIBUTION OF POWERS
	III	LEGISLATIVE DEPARTMENT
		LEGISLATIVE PROCEEDINGS
		LIMITATION ON LEGISLATIVE POWER
		STATE LOTTERY
		INITIATIVE AND REFERENDUM
	IV	EXECUTIVE DEPARTMENT
		REVENUE
		HIGHWAYS AND TRANSPORTATION
		AGRICULTURE
		ECONOMIC DEVELOPMENT
		INSURANCE
		SOCIAL SERVICES
		MENTAL HEALTH
		CONSERVATION
		NATURAL RESOURCES
		PUBLIC SAFETY
		LABOR AND INDUSTRIAL RELATIONS
		OFFICE OF ADMINISTRATION
		APPOINTMENT OF ADMINISTRATIVE HEADS
		HIGHER EDUCATION
		NONDISCRIMINATION IN APPOINTMENTS
	V	JUDICIAL DEPARTMENT
		SCHEDULE
	VI	LOCAL GOVERNMENT
		SPECIAL CHARTERS
		LOCAL GOVERNMENT
		FINANCES
		CITY AND COUNTY OF ST. LOUIS
		CITY OF ST. LOUIS
	VII	PUBLIC OFFICERS
	VIII	SUFFRAGE AND ELECTIONS
	IX	EDUCATION
	X	TAXATION
	XI	CORPORATIONS
		RAILROADS
		BANKS
	XII	AMENDING THE CONSTITUTION
		SCHEDULE
	XIII	PUBLIC EMPLOYEES

Source: RSMo, volume 20, page 41 (2000).

Begin your research by generating a list of descriptive words from the facts and issues of your problem. Search the indexes for your terms and record the references given. For example, under the term "Bingo," the General Index contains references to Article III, Section 39(a) of the Missouri Constitution, as well as to related statutes.

To find cases and other authorities that have discussed a certain provision of the Missouri Constitution, look at the brief summaries or *annotations* following the text of each section of the constitution in RSMo or VAMS. Annotations typically include a brief encapsulation of the court's holding regarding the constitutional section, with the case name, citation, date, and court. Some sections include quite a few annotations, while others have none. As a general rule, many more annotations will be available in VAMS than in RSMo. VAMS also includes references to historical notes, law review articles, and legal encyclopedias. To be sure you have the most current annotations, always check the pocket part. A *pocket part* is a paper supplement located in a pocket at the back of a print source. A pocket part will contain any new amendments and additional annotations since the bound volume was published.

The full text of the constitution is available on the state's website at www.moga.mo.gov/mostatutes/moconst.html. This site contains the text of the constitution with a table of contents.

B. Federal Constitution

The U.S. Constitution is published along with the Missouri Constitution in *Revised Statutes of Missouri*. An index immediately follows the text. No annotations are given in RSMo. The U.S. Constitution is also available in print in the first few volumes of *United States Code Annotated* and *United States Code Service*. Although these series are primarily used to research federal statutes, the publishers include the federal constitution as a convenience for researchers. These series are further discussed later in this chapter.

The U.S. Constitution is also available online at both state and federal government websites. Both Lexis Advance and WestlawNext include the U.S. Constitution in their databases.

II. Statutes

Statutes are a very important part of the American system of law. Most first-year law courses focus on appellate court decisions, or case law, with little attention paid to statutory law. However, citizens' lives are increasingly controlled by statutory law. For example, statutes govern the sale of goods, the requirements for certain professional licenses, and the disposition of property upon death. Case opinions are often judicial interpretations of statutes. "Most appellate court decisions, in fact, involve the application or interpretation of statutes rather than the consideration of common law principles."[8] If an applicable statute exists, then it becomes your main source of law, and the cases, if any, are used to interpret or supplement the statute.

There are both federal and state statutes. Federal statutes are created by the Congress of the United States pursuant to power emanating from the U.S. Constitution, and they apply nationally. State statutes are created by individual state legislatures and apply only in a particular state. If a conflict exists between a state statute and either the federal Constitution, a federal statute, or that state's constitution, then the federal law or the state constitution takes precedence.

A. Missouri Statutes

Statutes are compiled and indexed in two basic fashions—chronologically and topically (by subject matter). The actual wording of the statute appears in both the chronological and the topical compilations and in both print and online sources. While researchers usually begin looking for an appropriate governing statute by using the topical compilations (you will not likely know the date of enactment, which is needed to use the chronological compilations), it is important to understand chronological compilations as well.

1. Chronological Compilation — *Laws of Missouri*

A newly enacted statute is called a *session law* because it is passed during a legislative session. Missouri's chronological compilation of these new statutes is called *Laws of Missouri*. In general, new laws are not immediately published in a bound volume such as *Laws of Missouri*. Instead, they are first published as slip laws. A *slip law* is simply the paper pamphlet version of a law awaiting final publication. Missouri's version of a slip law is a "Truly Agreed to and Finally Passed" bill, which has been passed by both houses of the General Assembly of the State of Missouri but has not yet been signed by the Governor. Because the Governor has not yet signed this publication, technically it is not a law. Instead, the "Truly Agreed to and Finally Passed" bill is kept separately.

---

8. Morris L. Cohen & Kent C. Olson, *Legal Research in a Nutshell* 154 (11th ed. 2013).

To find a recently passed bill before its publication in the *Laws of Missouri*, you will need to know the bill number. Unfortunately, unless you have been following a particular bill for some reason, you will not likely have this information — chances are that at the start of your research you will not even know whether any relevant bills or statutes exist, let alone their reference numbers.

The session and slip laws are not very user-friendly. They are really only used to research the changes that have been made to legislation as it has progressed through the legislative process. That is, they are used to compare earlier versions of a bill with later versions of the law to see which sections have been enacted as proposed, amended, or deleted. Chapter 7 discusses how to research earlier versions of a bill as part of legislative history research. You cannot access a session law of Missouri without knowing the specific year in which the particular law was passed. Therefore, Missouri codifies its statutes to locate relevant sections more easily.

2. Topical Compilations — Missouri Codes

Because *Laws of Missouri* is arranged chronologically, it is almost impossible to use as a starting point unless you know which statute you are looking for and the date it was enacted by the General Assembly. Thus, a researcher needs a different tool to locate relevant statutes. That tool is called a *code*. A code organizes or "codifies" statutes by subject matter, rather than by the date on which the statute was enacted, and also provides an index to its codified statutes.

Some statutory codes are annotated. That is, they include references to other sources that cite or interpret particular code sections. For example, a statute's annotation may reference a case that interpreted that statute. Each annotation is written by the publisher of the code, not a legislature or a court. An annotation is intended to be an encapsulation of the main point from the part of the citing source that involved that particular code section. Publishers do not represent that the annotations provided in their annotated codes account for all existing citations to a statute. To find all citations to a statutory code, a researcher needs to use a citator. Citators are discussed in Chapter 5.

There are two codified versions of Missouri statutes, one official and one unofficial. The significant difference between official and unofficial codes is simply this: in the unlikely event that some discrepancy or difference exists between the official and unofficial versions of the statute, the official version controls and constitutes "the law." Rarely does a difference exist among the versions. Thus, for the most part, you can use whichever Missouri code you feel most comfortable with in your research. In court documents and memoranda, however, you should cite the official version whenever possible.

Missouri does not have an official rule on preferred citation of statutes. The two national citation manuals, *The Bluebook: A Uniform System of Citation*[9] and the *ALWD Citation Guide to Legal Citation*[10] state that Missouri statutes should be abbreviated as "Mo. Rev. Stat." or "Mo. Ann. Stat."[11] Missouri courts and practitioners universally use the designation "RSMo" as the abbreviation for the Missouri code, no matter which version of the code they use. In addition, Missouri practitioners and courts reverse the typical order of the statutory citation format: the section symbol and number are placed first, followed by the code abbreviation with no punctuation and ending with the date—for example, § 569.180 RSMo 2000.[12] Some Missouri practitioners and courts put the date in parentheses—§ 569.095 RSMo (Supp. 2014).[13] No Missouri statute or court rule dictates the use of RSMo, but not using it is a sure sign that an attorney is unfamiliar with Missouri practice. Citation is further explained in Appendix A.

a. Revised Statutes of Missouri

Missouri's official statutory publication, printed by the state, is called *Revised Statutes of Missouri*. Missouri also publishes an annual softbound cumulative supplement consisting of multiple volumes. Some of the volumes are pocket parts, placed in the back of each volume of RSMo. Others are kept separately.

Missouri statutes are also available online on both free and commercial websites. The free sites include sites sponsored by the General Assembly. One site allows the researcher to view the statutes, www.moga.mo.gov/mostatutes/statutesAna.html, while another provides full-text searching, www.moga.mo.gov/htmlpages2/statuteconstitutionsearch.aspx. The most popular commercial sites are WestlawNext and Lexis Advance. Both providers have numerous databases containing Missouri statutes. Missouri statutes are also available on Fastcase, a free service to all Missouri Bar members.

---

9. *The Bluebook: A Uniform System of Citation* (The Columbia Law Review et al. eds., 20th ed. 2015) (*Bluebook*).

10. ALWD & Coleen M. Barger, *ALWD Guide to Legal Citation* (5th ed. 2014) (*ALWD Guide*). Most citations in this book conform to the *ALWD Guide* and the *Bluebook*, except where there is a clear preference in Missouri for a different form.

11. Early printings of the fifth edition of the *ALWD Guide* contained an error.

12. The *Journal of The Missouri Bar* also utilizes this style of statutory citation. *See* The Missouri Bar, *Conventions for Citations*, J. of The Mo. Bar, http://mobar.org/uploadedFiles/Home/Publications/Journal/citations-conventions.pdf.

13. In a citation, "Supp." indicates that the statutory section cited is in the supplement or pocket part rather than the main volume.

One advantage to pulling up a statute or any source from a commercial on-line provider is that the document will contain hyperlinks so that you can move immediately to related authority to see if it is also helpful to your case. Statutory annotations include hyperlinks to allow easy movement to other sources. Citators are available immediately by clicking on the appropriate icon or tab, usually at the top of the document.

Missouri divides its statutes into chapters corresponding to subjects and sections corresponding to individual statutes. For example, the title of § 569.180 RSMo is:

Chapter 569 — Robbery, Arson, Burglary, and Related Offenses
Section 180 — Possession of burglar's tools

This is Missouri's statute regarding the crime of burglary using particular tools. Technically, RSMo is annotated, but the annotations are sparse. When RSMo does include an annotation, it is usually worth noting because it denotes something fundamentally important about interpreting that statute.

Unless you are doing historical research, you should always verify that you have the most recent statutory language. Updating is an essential component of all forms of legal research.

To update the text of § 569.180 in print sources, you must (1) look up the statute in the annual cumulative supplement and (2) look through any "Truly Agreed to and Finally Passed" bills to make sure there have not been any changes to the statute. Since the supplemental volumes are cumulative, you only need to look in the most current supplement. The older supplements are often kept on the library shelf in order to facilitate researching legislative history. To update further using the "Truly Agreed to" bills, you must know the bill number of any bill affecting your statute. Then you can look through the bills to find the status of your statute.

To update the text of § 569.180 online, the process is simplified. Online sources often provide the most current statutory language. Both WestlawNext and Lexis Advance have a feature that allows a researcher to locate pending legislation quickly. After locating the statute, click on "Proposed Legislation" on WestlawNext and "Pending Legislation" on Lexis Advance.

b. Vernon's Annotated Missouri Statutes

Missouri also has an unofficial, annotated version of its code, entitled *Vernon's Annotated Missouri Statutes* (VAMS), published by West. The format of VAMS is not the same as *Revised Statutes of Missouri*. The text of the statute itself is the same. The annotations, however, are much more extensive. VAMS also includes a section entitled "Comment" with each statute. In this comment section, West editors analyze the effect of the statute to assist the researcher in interpretation. VAMS also includes more research aids and references than RSMo does.

The process to update VAMS is similar to that of updating *Revised Statutes of Missouri*. VAMS (both the statute itself and the annotations) is updated by (1) the cumulative annual pocket part in the back of each volume and (2) pamphlets entitled *Vernon's Missouri Legislative Service*. If a statute has been enacted or amended subsequent to the publication of the hardbound VAMS volume, West publishes the new statutory text in the pocket part. The supplemental pamphlet is a chronological compilation of the newest Missouri laws. To update in the pamphlet, you must look at the "Statutes Amended, Repealed, Etc." table in the latest pamphlet. The table itself is cumulative even though the pamphlets are not. If a statute has been modified since the last VAMS pocket part, the statute's citation will appear in the table, and the table will note which pamphlet contains the text of the revision.

3. Applying Research Approaches

Although the code of Missouri is arranged by subject matter in both RSMo and VAMS, finding a particular statute is difficult unless you know its chapter number. Therefore, the Missouri code has index volumes at the end of each set. In order to solve a research problem using a Missouri index and code, you may use any of the three approaches introduced in Chapter 1. Likewise, all three approaches can be used in online sources.

a. Descriptive-Word Approach

The first step is to make a list of descriptive words that relate to the facts or legal issues in your problem. This step is explained in Chapter 1 for a client charged with possession of burglar tools for using a bent credit card. The descriptive words for that example are listed in Table 1-2. Choose the broadest word to begin your search and then use the more narrow words to look for subtopics under the broad word. While you are researching your words in an index, you might see other applicable words that you did not think of originally. You should add those words to your list.

The second step is to decide which jurisdiction's statutes govern your problem. Because burglary is controlled by state law and the client's actions all took place in Missouri, you should begin researching Missouri statutes. If you are ever in doubt about which jurisdiction's law applies, do some research in secondary sources first to get a generalized understanding of the area of law.

Figure 2-2. *Revised Statutes of Missouri* **General Index**

BURGLARY
   Boats, 569.160
   Church, 569.160
   Dwelling house, 569.160
   Explosives, penalty, 569.160
   First degree, penalty, 569.160
   Inhabitable structure, defined, 569.010
   Schoolhouse, 569.160
   Second degree, penalty, 569.170
   Tools, possession, penalty, 569.180
   Venue, 541.070
   Wrongfully taken, defined, 541.070

Source: RSMo, volume 16, page B-92 (2000).

Third, look up your descriptive words in the index to the Missouri code. Figure 2-2 illustrates an index section. You could use the index to either RSMo or VAMS. VAMS is the Missouri code used most often because of its extensive annotations. Begin by looking up the broadest word choice, "burglary." Then look for the other words on your descriptive-word list.

Jot down all relevant statutory citations listed. Before looking up the statutes, update the index by (1) looking in the pocket part to the index volume you are using and (2) looking in the subject index of any *Vernon's Missouri Legislative Service* supplement published since the pocket part. Remember the index in each supplement is *not* cumulative (although the table of statutes amended is), so you must look in each supplement.

The fourth step is to look up the statute referred to, § 569.180, in VAMS or RSMo (see Figure 2-3). This statute answers your question about whether a bent credit card is considered a "burglar tool." You now know that in Missouri any tool, instrument, or other article that has been adapted to use in a burglary may be considered a burglar tool. After the statutory language, you will find annotations leading to other sources of law.

Finally, update to make sure the statute has not changed since the bound copy of VAMS was published and to check for new annotations. First, check the pocket part in the back of the VAMS volume you are using. Next look for § 569.180 in the table of statutes amended in the most current *Vernon's Missouri Legislative Service* supplement. If the statute is listed, look up the change. If it is not, then § 569.180 is still good law.

Figure 2-3. *Vernon's Annotated Missouri Code* § 569.180 RSMo 2000

569.180. **Possession of burglar's tools**

1. A person commits the crime of possession of burglar's tools if he possesses any tool, instrument or other article adapted, designed or commonly used for committing or facilitating offenses involving forcible entry into premises, with a purpose to use or knowledge that some person has the purpose of using the same in making an unlawful forcible entry into a building or inhabitable structure or a room thereof.

2. Possession of burglar's tools is a class D felony.

(L.1977, S.B. No. 60, p. 662, § 1, eff. Jan. 1, 1979.)

Comment to 1973 Proposed Code

The section replaces § 560.115 RSMo and is based on New York Penal Code § 140.35. The section makes clear that purpose to use the tools for an unlawful entry of knowledge that someone else will so use them is required for guilt. This should require considerably more than simply evidence of prior arrests or reputation.

Historical and Statutory Notes

Prior Laws and Revisions:	R.S.1919, § 3306.
Mo.R.S.A. § 560.115.	R.S.1909, § 4529.
R.S.1939, § 4449.	R.S.1899, § 1892.
R.S.1929, § 4057.	

Source: Vernon's Annotated Missouri Statutes, volume 41, page 387 (2000). Reprinted with permission of Thomson Reuters..

After you have found a relevant statute, you should read the statutes surrounding it. Often, by reading the statutes codified before and after your statute, you can find a more applicable statute or an exception to your statute. You can also view the surrounding statutes when you have pulled up a statute with an online source by using the browsing function. This function allows you to move forward or backward throughout that chapter of statutes to view the surrounding sections. Use the annotations following your statute's text to find background information on the statute and to find other legal sources that have interpreted it. This background information may include citations to cases interpreting the statute, to applicable topics and key numbers, and to applicable administrative regulations.

Table 2-1 summarizes the descriptive-word approach for researching statutes in print sources.

Table 2-1. Descriptive-Word Approach to Statutory Research

1. Generate a list of descriptive words.
2. Determine which jurisdiction's statutes apply. The remaining steps assume Missouri is the jurisdiction.
3. Search the index of the statutory code for the descriptive words. Update this search by using the pocket parts of the index volumes and by checking *Vernon's Missouri Legislative Service.*
4. Read the potentially relevant statute and its surrounding statutes.
5. Review the outline of sections for that chapter for other possible statutes.
6. Update the statutes with pocket parts and by checking *Vernon's Missouri Legislative Service.*

Using the descriptive-word approach on WestlawNext or Lexis Advance, a researcher would construct a search query using the descriptive terms in any of several databases containing Missouri statutes. Then, features of each system allow you to perform the steps listed in Table 2-1.

b. Known-Topic Approach

The known-topic approach to research is used when the researcher can specify the topic without first searching any indexes. A researcher experienced in a topic area understands the terms of art and may have already researched similar topics on numerous occasions. As a result, that researcher can move directly to the applicable topic. Each chapter of the Missouri code begins with an outline of the sections of that chapter. The researcher can peruse that outline in print or online to find the applicable statutory sections.

A less-experienced researcher may also use the known-topic approach after discerning applicable terms of art and gaining a general understanding of the topic. Frequently, the known-topic approach will be used as a check to find other applicable statutes after the less-experienced researcher locates an initial statutory section using the descriptive-word approach.

c. Known-Authority Approach

A researcher who knows an applicable statutory section can short-cut the search of the index and outline and move directly to the statute. Legislative acts are often given popular names, either by the sponsors of the bill or by the press. If you only know the statute by its popular name, the General Index contains a Popular Name Table that converts the popular name to its corresponding statutory code.

To use the known-authority approach in an online database, a researcher can enter the statute's citation in a search box near the top of the screen on both Lexis Advance and on WestlawNext.

Armed with the applicable statute, you can use its annotations to find judicial opinions interpreting the statute's language. Then you can browse the outline of sections and browse the surrounding statutes for other applicable statutes, definitions, or exceptions.

B. Federal Statutes

1. Chronological Compilations

a. United States Statutes at Large

The official, government-published, chronological compilation of federal statutes is the *United States Statutes at Large*. These statutes are known as "session laws" because they are passed during a congressional session. *Statutes at Large* (cited as "Stat.") is published annually by the federal government and contains all of the statutes passed by the Congress during that annual session. Volumes are arranged and numbered chronologically by congressional session. The volume numbers no longer match the number of the congressional session. For example, the laws of the first session of the 112th Congress, which met in 2011, are contained in volume 125 of *Statutes at Large* and the laws of the second session of the 112th Congress, which met in 2012, are contained in volume 126. It often takes more than one book to house all of the laws passed during one congressional session. Therefore, several books might have the same volume number.

A citation to *Statutes at Large* consists of the volume number and the page number of the applicable text. For example, 124 Stat. 244 refers to the statute in volume 124 of *Statutes at Large* starting on page 244. In addition, each statute is assigned a public law number for identification purposes. The public law number can be found at the top of each page in *Statutes at Large*. For example, the Patient Protection and Affordable Care Act, commonly known as the Affordable Care Act, is Public Law 111-148. The first number, 111, designates the number of the Congress that enacted the legislation (in this case, the 111th Congress), and the second number indicates that this was the 148th law passed by the 111th Congress. The public law number is the one number that is used to refer to the entire act, while the *Statutes at Large* citation (124 Stat. 244) will be different for each page of the statute. Therefore, the Requirements to Maintain Minimal Essential Coverage, Section 1501, of the Affordable Care Act would be cited as 124 Stat. 244, while the Act in its entirety can be cited as Public Law 111-148.

Within each volume of *Statutes at Large*, the statutes are arranged sequentially in order of their public law number. Only the text of the statute as it was originally adopted is printed in *Statutes at Large*. There is not a supplemental pocket part to update the text located in the back of any volume of *Statutes at Large*. That is because the text in any volume will never be changed or updated. If and when Congress passes an amendment to a statute, the amendment will get its own public law number and will be compiled sequentially with all of the other laws passed during that session of Congress.

Since *Statutes at Large* is a chronological compilation of laws passed by Congress during an annual session, and since it contains nothing more than the original text of the law, it generally is not very helpful to a beginning researcher and is definitely not the best place to start your statutory research if you do not know whether or when a statute was enacted. *Statutes at Large* is used by lawyers or other researchers who are attempting to (1) determine the Congress's intent by looking at the statute's original language, (2) review the whole body of congressional action for a given session, or (3) locate some congressional action that does not appear in a subject matter compilation of federal statutes.

b. United States Code Congressional and Administrative News

The unofficial, commercially published chronological compilation of federal statutes is the *United States Code Congressional and Administrative News* (U.S.C.C.A.N.) (pronounced "u-scan") published by West. Like *Statutes at Large*, U.S.C.C.A.N. also contains all laws produced in a congressional session. Additionally, U.S.C.C.A.N. provides a detailed (although incomplete) legislative history of each statute, often including a copy of the House or Senate report. Unfortunately, U.S.C.C.A.N. has no cumulative general subject index; it only has a subject index in the last volume of each year for the subjects covered in the volumes of that year. Therefore, as with *Statutes at Large*, a researcher would need to know at least the year in which a statute was enacted in order to find it by subject in a U.S.C.C.A.N. index. Also, like *Statutes at Large*, U.S.C.C.A.N. contains only the original text of the statute. Any later amendments or changes will be found under their own public law number in another volume. As a result, U.S.C.C.A.N. is not widely used in initial research to find an on point statute but rather is more commonly used for researching the legislative history of a known statute.

2. Topical Compilations — Federal Codes

a. United States Code

The official code, published by the federal government, is entitled the *United States Code* (U.S.C.). The federal government reissues a new edition of U.S.C. every six years. Between editions, the volumes are updated by bound supplements. The supplements are cumulative; thus, in order to update U.S.C., you need only look in the latest supplement. Because U.S.C. is slow to be published, however, it is rarely the best place to find the current language of a federal statute. Unofficial codes, discussed below, are often better research tools.

U.S.C. is organized by general subject matter or topic.[14] All of the statutes dealing with one subject, no matter when they were enacted by Congress, are grouped together under one "title." U.S.C. is currently divided into fifty-two such titles.[15] Each of the fifty-two titles is divided into chapters (each chapter is concerned with a specific act), and then into sections (each section covers one statute within the act). For example, 26 U.S.C. § 5000A is:

> Title 26 — Internal Revenue Code
> > Subtitle D — Miscellaneous Excise Taxes
> > > Chapter 48 — Maintenance of Minimum Essential Coverage
> > > > Section 5000A — Requirements to Maintain Minimum
> > > > Essential Coverage

This is the codified form of the Affordable Care Act. U.S.C., like the two unofficial codes, differs from *Statutes at Large* in that amendments are incorporated into the original text and repealed laws are deleted from the compilation. That is one research advantage of codified statutes over chronological compilations. A researcher saves time by not having to look up each amendment.

The text, of course, does not reflect any judicial decisions that may have affected the statute's interpretation and application in a certain jurisdiction. If, for example, a U.S. Supreme Court case had found the statute to be unconstitutional, that decision would not be reflected in the text of this version of

---

14. Titles 1–5 address the organization of government. Title 6 is Domestic Security. Titles 7–50 are alphabetical, with the exception of Title 38, Veterans' Benefits. Title 51-52 were recently authorized and cover National and Commercial Space Programs, and Voting and Elections.

15. The Office of Law Revision Counsel of the United States House of Representatives has drafted legislation to expand the number of titles to fifty-five. Fifty-four titles have now been created, although one is empty and another is reserved.

the codified statute. Unofficial versions of federal statutes include reference to cases in their annotations.

At the end of the text of a section, before the section entitled "References in Text," is the *Statutes at Large* citation and public law number for each statute. This can be very helpful information if a researcher needs to see the text of an original statute before it was changed by any amendments.

U.S.C. also has several helpful tables, such as a *Statutes at Large* conversion table, which converts the chronological acts of Congress to their codified U.S.C. sections, and a public law number conversion table, which converts the public law number to its codified U.S.C. section. The "Acts Cited by Popular Name" table is an alphabetical listing of acts by their commonly used names and provides the U.S.C. citation and public law number for the acts. U.S.C. also has a large general index.

The only step to updating U.S.C. in print is to consult the most current annual bound supplement. Since the supplements are cumulative, you need only consult the most recent volumes. There may not yet be an annual supplement to U.S.C. at the time you are doing your research. Like Missouri statutes in an online source, federal statutes in online sources usually contain the most current language.

Because the U.S.C. is somewhat slow in its publication schedule, it is often necessary to consult the privately published, unofficial code publications. The two unofficial codifications of federal statutes are the *United States Code Annotated* and the *United States Code Service*.

b. United States Code Annotated

United States Code Annotated (U.S.C.A.) is published by West. In addition to the codified statutes, West provides citations to case decisions and secondary sources that will lead the researcher to other sources of law that interpret a given statute. The U.S.C.A. organizes statutes exactly like the official U.S.C. Therefore, the Affordable Care Act can be found in both sources beginning at Title 26, Section 5000A.

At the beginning of the statute is an outline of the individual statutes or sections of an act. Following the outline is a section entitled "Cross References" where you can find other topics that might be related to the act.

Statutory text in U.S.C.A. is identical to that in U.S.C. After each code section, West's U.S.C.A. provides several forms of annotations to help a researcher interpret the statute.

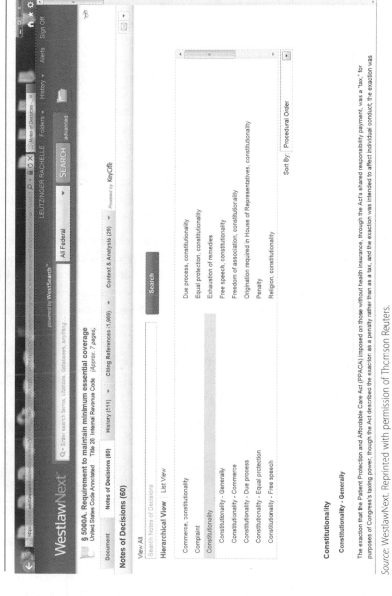

Figure 2-4. 26 U.S.C.A. § 5000A Index of Notes of Decisions on WestlawNext

- **Historical and Statutory Notes**—These are notes of amendments to the statute and the legislative history of the statute, including citations to West's U.S.C.C.A.N.

- **Cross References**—This section points to other statutes that might be helpful to understanding the statute.

- *American Law Reports*—This section lists any available annotations in the secondary source *American Law Reports*, which contains both the full text of selected cases and commentary on issues presented by those cases.

- **Library References**—This section provides citations to applicable administrative agency regulations that might affect or help to implement the statute. Administrative agency regulations are covered in Chapter 4. In addition, West topics and key numbers that correspond to the subject of the statute are given; these research tools are useful for finding cases on point. They are explained in Chapter 3, which covers case reporters and digests. Also found under Library References are citations to secondary sources published by West. Secondary sources are helpful when learning the basics of a subject, as discussed in Chapter 6.

- **Notes of Decisions**—This section contains notes and annotations and is probably the most helpful of all of the research aids because it leads directly to cases interpreting the statute. Each note or annotation briefly describes the case it refers to and provides a citation. An index at the beginning of this section arranges the notes and annotations by subject. When there are only a few case annotations, it is easy to read each of them and the index seems unimportant. However, when there are numerous annotations, it is often faster to look for a topic in the index rather than to read all of the annotations. Figure 2-4 displays this annotation index of 26 U.S.C.A. § 5000A.

U.S.C.A. has a general index to the entire code, an individual index to each title, and several volumes of tables. The table volumes contain many of the same conversion tables found in U.S.C.

To update a statute as published in a print volume of U.S.C.A., consult (1) the pocket part in the back of the U.S.C.A. volume that you are using and (2) any U.S.C.A. interim pamphlet supplement issued after the pocket part.

Some legal researchers prefer to use U.S.C.A. because of its annotations to cases and its integration with the West topic and key number system. U.S.C.A. is available only on WestlawNext. Other researchers prefer the other unofficial, privately published annotated code, *United States Code Service*, which is integrated with Lexis Advance, West's primary competitor in legal publishing.

c. United States Code Service

United States Code Service (U.S.C.S.) is organized in the same fashion as U.S.C. and U.S.C.A., using the same fifty-two titles. U.S.C.S. has many of the same annotations following the text of the statute as does U.S.C.A.: History, *Code of Federal Regulations*, Cross References, Research Guide, and Interpretive Notes and Decisions. U.S.C.S. also has some features not found in U.S.C.A. For example, instead of West topics and key numbers and citations to West secondary sources, U.S.C.S. provides citations to other secondary sources including *American Jurisprudence* and law review articles.

The U.S.C.S. Interpretive Notes and Decisions section includes both judicial decisions (made by a court) and some administrative agency decisions (made by agencies' administrative law judges), while the U.S.C.A. Notes of Decisions section includes only judicial decisions.

In addition to the conversion and popular name tables, U.S.C.S. includes many "Court Rules" volumes following the fifty-two titles of the code. These volumes annotate both the Federal Rules of Civil Procedure and the Federal Rules of Criminal Procedure.[16] Additional volumes contain both rules of procedure and interpretive notes for federal administrative agencies such as the Internal Revenue Service, Federal Communications Commission, and Federal Trade Commission.

To update U.S.C.S. in print, consult (1) the annual pocket part (called a "cumulative supplement") in the back of the U.S.C.S. volume that you are using and (2) the "Table of Code Sections Added, Amended, Repealed, or Otherwise Affected" in the most recent monthly U.S.C.S. *Advance Service* pamphlet. Although U.S.C.S. *Advance Service* pamphlets themselves are not cumulative, this table is cumulative, so a researcher only needs to look in the most current month available. If the statute has been affected since publication of the annual pocket part, the title and section will appear in the table along with the public law number. A researcher can then look up the public law number in the appropriate *Advance Service* pamphlet.

3. Applying Research Approaches

a. Descriptive-Word Approach

The descriptive-word approach begins with making a list of descriptive words that might lead you to an applicable statute. Next, look up the descriptive

---

16. For example, U.S.C.A. integrates the Federal Rules of Criminal Procedure with Title 18.

words in the appropriate index. The official U.S.C. provides only a general subject index, while U.S.C.A. and U.S.C.S. each provide both a general subject index and an individual index to each title. The index to an individual title is located in the last volume of that title.

Update this index search to make sure that you have found all of the applicable topical references to statutes by checking the interim pamphlet supplements. Look in all interim pamphlet supplements to see if any new laws have been passed that might affect your problem. The index is in the very back of each supplement and will generally consist of only a few pages.

Now use the references listed in the index to look up the statutes in a code. View the surrounding statute sections. Finally, update your research to make sure that there have been no changes to the statutory language since the bound copy of U.S.C., U.S.C.A., or U.S.C.S. you are using was published. Some researchers will actually check the pocket part first to be sure they have the most current language.

b. Known-Topic Approach

At the beginning of each title and at the beginning of each chapter in U.S.C., U.S.C.A., and U.S.C.S., an outline of the code sections is available. The researcher who already understands her topic can move directly to this outline to locate the applicable code section and related materials.

c. Known-Authority Approach

In addition to using a statute's citation to pull the statute directly, you may also use the known-authority approach if you have the *Statutes at Large* citation to a relevant statute. You can use the tables in U.S.C., U.S.C.A., or U.S.C.S. to convert that information into the applicable statutory code section. If you only know the popular name of an act, you may use the "Acts Cited by Popular Name" table in U.S.C. or similar tables in U.S.C.A. and U.S.C.S. to learn the citation.

4. Online Sources

Statutory codes are widely available online. Descriptive-word searches in full-text databases lead to current versions of applicable statutes. The federal government sponsors both http://uscode.house.gov and www.gpo.gov/fdsys/browse/collectionUScode.action?collectionCode =USCODE. Cornell Legal Information Institute sponsors www.law cornell.edu/uscode/text, a reputable academic site.

III. Summary

The Missouri and federal constitutions are the supreme sources of primary authority. Like the constitutions of other states, Missouri's constitution is detailed and at times statutory in nature. Fortunately, using the general index of a Missouri statutory code will guide the Missouri researcher to relevant constitutional provisions.

Missouri and federal statutes are compiled in two fashions: chronologically and topically. The chronological compilations are referred to as session laws. Session laws are updated by individual paperback slip laws until the bound version is published. Chronological compilations of statutes are not very helpful to the legal researcher unless she knows the specific year in which a law was passed by the legislature. Session laws are mainly used for legislative history research.

The topical compilation of statutes is called a code or codification. Codes are arranged by subject matter. All statutes relating to one broad subject are grouped together in one division of the code. The text of the statutes found in the code reflects any amendments or revisions made to the original statute. A code is accessible in print through its general index. By looking up descriptive words in the index to a code, a researcher is led to applicable statutes. Often codes are annotated. Annotations provide references to other authority that may interpret the statutory provision. Most print codes are updated with annual pocket parts and periodic paperback supplements. Online versions of statutes already contain the most current language.

Chapter 3

Case Reporters and Digests

Common law is judge-made law. This judge-made law applies particularly to the parties to the case or dispute immediately before the court and may also apply to other, similarly situated parties who may have a similar dispute in the future.

Case law generally refers to the aggregate body of prior court decisions. These previously decided cases are called *precedent*. In order to advise a client, a lawyer will research and refer to precedent to learn how prior courts have decided similar questions or legal issues in the past. The lawyer can be somewhat confident that a court will attempt to follow earlier decisions or cases in later, similar situations because of the doctrine of *stare decisis*. The doctrine of *stare decisis* compels courts to abide by or adhere to previously decided cases. The practical effect of *stare decisis* is to give lawyers and citizens the confidence that similarly situated persons are treated the same under the law.

Case decisions are compiled somewhat chronologically in *reporters*. The common method of access to reporters is through topical or subject-matter indexing provided by case *digests*. This chapter explains how court systems are structured, how case law is reported and updated in the United States, and how to find cases within the reporter system by using print digests and online databases.

I. Court Systems

Because much legal research includes reading judicial opinions, researchers need to understand the court system of the law they are applying. The basic court structure includes a trial court, an intermediate court of appeals, and a court of last resort, often called the "supreme" court.[1] This structure exists at both the state and federal levels.

---

1. For brevity, the following description omits local courts. Information on these courts is available on the state's website at www.mo.gov, under the "Government" drop-

A. Missouri Courts

In Missouri, the trial courts are called circuit courts. These courts exist in each of Missouri's 114 counties,[2] plus the City of St. Louis. Missouri has one intermediate appellate court, the Missouri Court of Appeals. This court sits in three districts, designated by each district's jurisdiction. The Missouri Court of Appeals, Western District sits primarily in Kansas City. The Missouri Court of Appeals, Eastern District sits primarily in St. Louis, and the Missouri Court of Appeals, Southern District regularly hears cases in Springfield and in Poplar Bluff. Each district of the Court of Appeals is composed of seven to fourteen judges, who sit in three-judge panels. Circuit courts in Missouri are bound by the decisions of all districts of the Missouri Court of Appeals, not just the one within their geographical boundary.[3] The Supreme Court of Missouri, which is constitutionally mandated to sit in Jefferson City, has seven judges.[4] The seven judges sit *en banc* to hear all cases, unless a judge is recused.

The website for the Missouri judiciary is www.courts.mo.gov. It contains a wealth of information, including a listing of Missouri's circuit courts, links to courts maintaining websites, useful forms, lists of court personnel and contact information, and recent opinions of the appellate courts.

B. Federal Courts

In the federal judicial system, the trial courts are called United States District Courts. There are ninety-four district courts in the federal system, with each district drawn from a particular state. States with larger populations and higher caseloads are subdivided into more districts. Missouri is divided into two federal districts, eastern and western.[5] The court in each district is typically located in more than one city. For example, the United States District Court

---

down box, "Judicial Branch" link, then the "Municipal Courts" link.

2. The state is divided into forty-five judicial circuits; each circuit includes one to five counties. The City of St. Louis is an independent city, not part of a county, but is the Twenty-Second Judicial Circuit Court.

3. *Akins v. Dir. of Revenue*, 303 S.W.3d 563, 567 n.4 (Mo. 2010).

4. In some jurisdictions, a jurist on the highest court is called a "justice," while on lower courts the term "judge" is used. In Missouri all jurists are referred to as judges, except for the chief justice of the Supreme Court of Missouri.

5. The two federal districts do not correspond to the three different Missouri Court of Appeals' divisions. This situation can be confusing. The Missouri Court of Appeals, Western District does not cover the exact same geographical territory as the United States District Court for the Western District of Missouri. The same is true for the Missouri Court of Appeals, Eastern District and the United States District Court for the Eastern District of Missouri.

for the Western District of Missouri is located not only in Kansas City but also in Jefferson City and Springfield. A state with a relatively small population may not be subdivided into smaller geographic regions. The entire state of Kansas, for example, comprises the United States District Court for the District of Kansas. Even so, divisions of the federal district court are located in three Kansas cities: Kansas City, Topeka, and Wichita.

Intermediate appellate courts in the federal system are called United States Courts of Appeals. There are courts of appeals for each of the thirteen federal circuits. Twelve of these circuits are based on geographic jurisdiction. Eleven numbered circuits cover all the states, with the twelfth being the District of Columbia Circuit. The thirteenth federal circuit, called the Federal Circuit, hears appeals from district courts in all other circuits on issues related to patent law and cases arising from certain specialized courts and agencies. A map showing the federal circuits is available at www.uscourts.gov/court_locator.aspx. Circuit maps may also be found in the front of the *Federal Supplement* and the *Federal Reporter*, books that publish the cases decided by federal courts.

Missouri is in the Eighth Circuit of the United States Court of Appeals. This means that cases from the United States District Court for both the Eastern and Western Districts of Missouri are appealed to the United States Court of Appeals for the Eighth Circuit. This circuit encompasses Arkansas, Iowa, Minnesota, Missouri, Nebraska, North Dakota, and South Dakota.

The highest court in the federal system is the United States Supreme Court. It decides cases concerning the United States Constitution and federal statutes. This court does not have the final say on matters of purely state law; that authority rests with the highest court of each state. If the question is one of federal law, however, the decisions of the U.S. Supreme Court are binding on the state courts. For example, if the U.S. Supreme Court holds that a Missouri statute violates the U.S. Constitution, that decision is binding on state courts. Parties who wish to have the U.S. Supreme Court hear their case must file a petition for *certiorari*, as the court has discretion over which cases it hears.

The website for the federal judiciary contains maps, court addresses, explanations of jurisdiction, and other helpful information. The address is www.uscourts.gov/Home.aspx.

C. Courts of Other States

Most states have a three-tier court system like that of Missouri. A few states do not have an intermediate appellate court. Another difference in some court systems is that the "supreme" court is not the highest court. In New York, the trial courts are called supreme courts, and the highest court is the Court of Appeals. Two other states, Massachusetts and Maine, call their highest court the Supreme Judicial Court.

II. Reporters

In order for our precedent-based, common law system to function, judges, attorneys, and potential litigants must have a way to learn how similar situations have been treated and resolved previously by courts. This is accomplished through a series of books called *reporters*, which contain the collection of case opinions decided and designated for publication by the various courts.

There are both official and unofficial reporters. *Official reporters* are typically published by state and federal governments. Historically, a significant lag time occurred between when a court rendered a decision and when that decision was published in the official reporter of that court. To remedy this situation, the West Publishing Company devised a system of *unofficial reporters* that covers all of the state and federal courts in the American legal system. This system is called the National Reporter System. These unofficial reporters proved accurate and timely. Often, a court's written decision or opinion in a case will appear in *both* an official reporter and an unofficial West reporter. Sometimes, a court's decision will appear only in a West reporter; this occurs when a state government stops publishing its own reports. When this occurs, the West reporter becomes the official print reporter.

The National Reporter System divides the fifty states into seven regions. Each region has a separate reporter that contains judicial opinions from the states' highest courts and intermediate courts of appeal.[6] The seven regions are Atlantic, North Eastern, North Western, Pacific, Southern, South Eastern, and South Western.

Each reporter in the National Reporter System has been issued in more than one series. Each series covers a specific time span. When locating a specific opinion, whether in print or online, you need to be sure to have the correct series. For example, *South Western Reporter* is now in its third series. The first series covers decisions from 1886 to 1927. The second series covers 1927 to 1999. The third series began in 1999 and includes current decisions.

---

6. West also publishes separate reporters for New York and California intermediate appellate court decisions, which are not then included in the regional reporters.

A. Missouri Judicial Opinions

Recent Missouri court opinions are published in West's *South Western Reporter*. There has not been a governmentally-published reporter for Missouri opinions since 1956. This does not mean that the official reporter is the only place one can locate a written case report. Missouri decisions are also available online through WestlawNext, Lexis Advance, and Fastcase and on the Missouri judiciary's website, www.courts.mo.gov.

Not all court decisions are published in print. It is largely up to the court itself to decide which decisions or opinions are published and which will be sent only to the parties involved. Because appellate court decisions are binding on the lower courts within that jurisdiction, they must be accessible to attorneys and judges. Therefore, almost all appellate court decisions in every jurisdiction are published. For example, all of the United States Supreme Court opinions are published. Each state publishes its highest court's opinions in its own reporters, in the West regional reporter, or in both the state and the West reporters.

Cases heard by the lower state courts are not often published. These court decisions are not published in a reporter unless the judge thinks that new or groundbreaking law has been made by those trial court decisions. Online publishers, however, do include some of these unpublished opinions in their databases. Be cautious in citing to this authority as some courts do not recognize unpublished opinions as having any precedential value and prohibit their use.[7]

The process of publication is simple. When an appellate court hands down a decision, the parties are each sent a copy. Other copies of that decision are transmitted to both West and the official reporting company, if one exists in that jurisdiction. The case decisions are printed in roughly chronological order in the appropriate West unofficial reporter volume and in any official reporter volume. Each case is assigned an "address" or citation for each particular reporter where it is located. An opinion published in both an official and an unofficial reporter will have two "addresses" or citations. For example, *State v. Lake* is a case decided by the Missouri Court of Appeals, Eastern District. Missouri opinions are only available in printed version in *South Western Reporter* and thus have only one citation or address, 686 S.W.2d 19. If, instead, a Kansas

---

7. *See* 8th Cir. R. 32.1A ("Unpublished opinions are decisions which a court designates for unpublished status. They are not precedent.... Unpublished opinions issued before January 1, 2007, generally should not be cited.").

court had decided the case, it would be available in two reporters: an official reporter published by the state, *Kansas Reports* or *Kansas Court of Appeals Reports*, and an unofficial regional reporter published by West called the *Pacific Reporter*. Therefore, *Libel v. Corcoran*, a Kansas Supreme Court opinion, has two addresses or citations: 203 Kan. 181 (the official reporter) and 452 P.2d 832 (the unofficial West reporter). The same Kansas Supreme Court opinion is published in both reporters. These two addresses are called *parallel citations*.

Because Missouri appellate decisions are published only in the West reporter, this book concentrates on that format of reporting cases. Each case contains several parts. The following discussion looks in detail at the *State v. Lake* case reported at 686 S.W.2d 19. Refer to the case excerpts in Figures 3-1 through 3-3 as these parts are explained.

1. Citation

A case citation allows anyone who sees the citation to find that specific case. The citation consists of the volume number of the reporter, the reporter series, and the page number on which the case begins. In this example, the citation of the *Lake* case is 686 S.W.2d 19. The case appears in volume 686 of the *South Western Reporter, Second Series*, beginning at page 19. As you can see from Figure 3-1, the opinion in *Lake* was handed down on December 26, 1984,[8] by the Missouri Court of Appeals, Eastern District. The citation that appears in the reporter forms the basis for the citation format that attorneys use in documents.

Online sources use the same citation to locate a published decision in their databases. For unpublished decisions, online providers use a citation address unique to their systems that at a minimum includes the docket number, the date of the decision, and the court.

2. Caption

The case caption appears at the beginning of the case and states the names of the parties involved in the suit. The full name of the *Lake* case, including all of its parties, is rather long. Notice, however, that the words "State" and "Lake" are in all capital letters. This font indicates the words that are to be used when the case name is cited in text or a footnote.

---

8. The case opinion may include other dates of motions and petitions made after the decision was rendered. These dates may be important when updating the law. For citation, only the date of decision is used.

Figure 3-1. *State v. Lake,* 686 S.W.2d 19, Caption and Synopsis

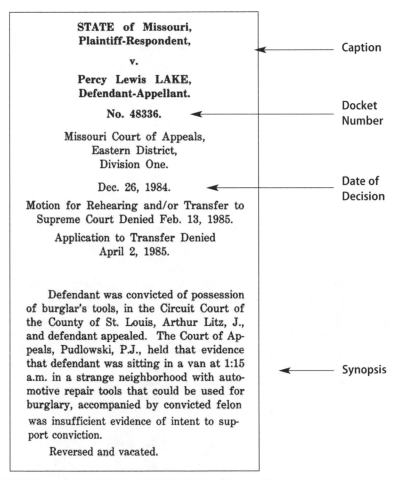

STATE of Missouri,
Plaintiff-Respondent,

v.

Percy Lewis LAKE,
Defendant-Appellant.

◄——— Caption

No. 48336. ◄

◄——— Docket Number

Missouri Court of Appeals,
Eastern District,
Division One.

Dec. 26, 1984. ◄

◄——— Date of Decision

Motion for Rehearing and/or Transfer to
Supreme Court Denied Feb. 13, 1985.

Application to Transfer Denied
April 2, 1985.

Defendant was convicted of possession
of burglar's tools, in the Circuit Court of
the County of St. Louis, Arthur Litz, J.,
and defendant appealed. The Court of Appeals, Pudlowski, P.J., held that evidence
that defendant was sitting in a van at 1:15
a.m. in a strange neighborhood with auto-
motive repair tools that could be used for
burglary, accompanied by convicted felon
was insufficient evidence of intent to support conviction.

Reversed and vacated.

◄——— Synopsis

Source: South Western Reporter 2d. Reprinted with permission of Thomson Reuters.

The party or parties that appear before the "v." are often, but not always, the plaintiffs, and the party or parties appearing after the "v." are usually the defendants. Historically, courts modified the names on appeal to list the party appealing the decision (the appellant) first and the appellee second. Most courts no longer follow this practice; now, the plaintiff remains the first-listed party regardless of who is appealing. In *Lake*, the State of Missouri was the original plaintiff (through a county prosecutor). Percy Lake, the defendant, was the one appealing the trial court's decision.

Figure 3-2. *State v. Lake*, 686 S.W.2d 19,
Headnotes in Print Decision

1. Burglary ☞12
　　Actual physical possession is not required to convict person of the crime of
possession of burglar's tools; joint possession is sufficient. V.A.M.S. § 569.180.

2. Burglary ☞12 ◄———————————— Topic
　　Fact that tools were on the floor of a　　　and Key
van and were highly visible was sufficient　Number
for jury to conclude that driver had posses-
sion, for purposes of prosecuting driver for ◄——— Headnote
possession of burglar's tools. V.A.M.S.
§ 569.180.

3. Burglary ☞12
　　For purposes of statute prohibiting
possession of burglar's tools, it is immateri-
al that tools are designed and adapted for
lawful use; if state proves that tools are
suitable for illegal purposes, they are "burglar's tools." V.A.M.S. § 569.180.
　　　See publication Words and Phrases
　　　for other judicial constructions and
　　　definitions.

4. Burglary ☞12
　　Fact that pry bars and wire cutters
could be adapted for illegitimate use established that they were "burglar's tools."
V.A.M.S. § 569.180.

Source: South Western Reporter 2d. Reprinted with permission of Thomson Reuters.

3. Docket Number

Immediately below the case name is the docket number of the case. The docket number for *State v. Lake* is No. 48336. This docket number is assigned by the Clerk of the Court and is used to identify all papers submitted to that particular court regarding the case. The docket number may be needed as a reference if requesting court documents for the case from the clerk's office or if using an online provider's citation format.

Figure 3-3. *State v. Lake*, 686 S.W.2d 19,
Headnotes on WestlawNext

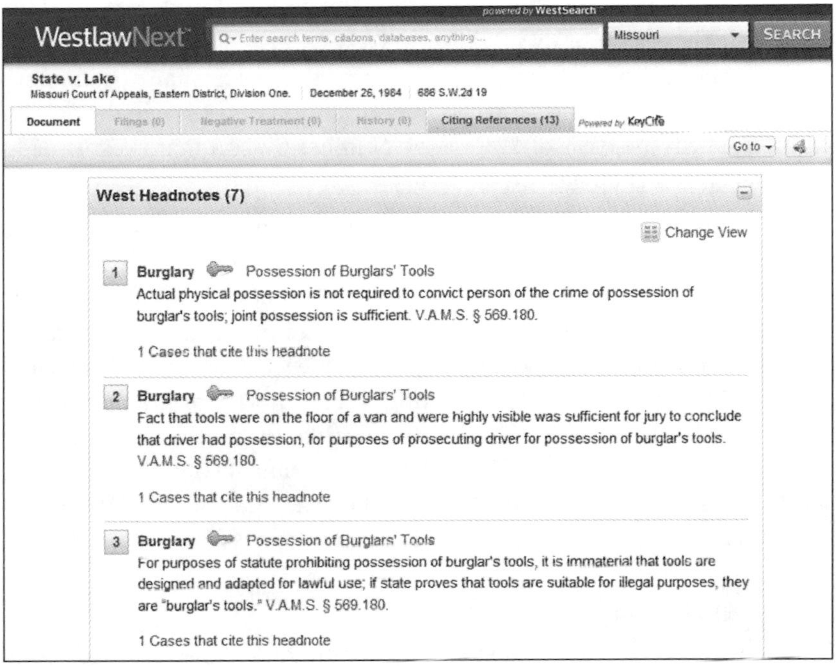

Source: WestlawNext. Reprinted with permission of Thomson Reuters.

4. Synopsis

Following the name of the court issuing the opinion and the date the opinion was issued is a paragraph briefly summarizing both the procedural posture of the case and its holding. This synopsis is written by West editors to give an overview of the case; it is not part of the court's opinion and therefore cannot be relied upon as authority.[9]

5. Headnotes

Following the synopsis are short, numbered paragraphs known as *headnotes*, shown in Figures 3-2 and 3-3. Headnotes are an editorial feature written by

---

9. Some courts, but not Missouri courts, draft their own synopses or syllabi. Indeed, Kansas statutes mandate that the Kansas Supreme Court issue a syllabus of the case. Kan. Stat. Ann. §§ 20–111, 60-2106 (2015). Those summaries appear after the headnotes at the beginning of the text of the opinion. Court-drafted syllabi are frequently cited by Kansas courts as authority, but other courts typically do not cite syllabi.

the West editors. They consist of a brief statement of the facts and a brief statement of the rule of law that the court applied to those facts to reach its decision. Each headnote reflects a single point of law. Legal issues are never combined within a single headnote. Note that the West editors refer you to applicable statutes at the end of each headnote. A case will have as many headnotes as the editorial staff determines there are important points of law in the opinion. Headnotes form the basis of West's Key Number System that is explained in detail later in this chapter.

Each headnote is systematically numbered and classified by West according to the area of law discussed by the corresponding part of the court's opinion. The headnotes themselves provide a quick preview of a case, but they are not a substitute for the case decision. Because headnotes are written by West editors, not by the court, they carry no authoritative value whatsoever and thus should not be relied upon or cited as case authority. Headnotes are strictly a research aid provided by the West editors to help researchers find the applicable parts of a decision. In Figures 3-2 and 3-3, headnotes 3 and 4 contain points of law regarding possession of burglar's tools. In the text, the symbols [3][4] refer to headnotes 3 and 4, directing you to the text that relates to those headnotes.

6. Attorneys and Judges

Immediately preceding the text of the full opinion are the names of counsel (the lawyers) for each of the parties to the action and the cities where they practice. Below the names of the attorneys is the name of the judge (or judges) who delivered the court's opinion in the case.

7. Opinion of the Court

In a West-reported case, the opinion is the only portion that was written by the judge. The opinion begins after the judge's name. The opinion contains the legal reasoning and decision of the court after hearing the case either at trial or on a dispositive motion, or, in the case of an appellate court, after reading the appellate briefs and hearing oral arguments of counsel. A case opinion usually summarizes key facts. In addition, appellate court opinions usually include a brief history of the lower court's ruling and legal reasoning.

Appellate court opinions may not be unanimous and often contain dissenting and concurring opinions. Dissenting opinions are written by one or more judges who disagree with the majority decision. Concurring opinions are written by one or more judges who agree with the ultimate decision or result of the majority but for different or additional reasons. These opinions are located immediately after the text of the majority opinion.

The holding of the majority opinion is the text that lawyers and other courts may quote or cite as precedent. Often the holding of the case will be very narrow and direct, but in the process of delivering the holding, the court will expound on the legal reasoning it used to reach its decision. You cannot tell what the real holding of the court is until you read the entire opinion.

Sometimes the court explains what might happen when its holding is applied to different facts. For example, the court might state which it would not reach the same conclusion on different facts. This part of the case opinion is called *dicta* and does not carry any binding authority. Only the actual holding of the case is binding precedent that must be followed by lower courts within the jurisdiction. The dicta of a case can be valuable to a researcher, however, especially in an area of underdeveloped law. If a researcher's facts are similar to the facts in dicta, the court's thoughts and reasoning would be very helpful in predicting which direction the court would follow in ruling on the new facts. Be careful, however, to rely only on the holding when quoting or restating what the law presently is.

8. Disposition

The disposition is the final decision rendered by the court. It typically appears at or very near the end of the opinion. In the case of an appellate court opinion that contains a dissenting opinion, the disposition will appear at the end of the majority opinion. The decision of a trial court will often designate either "judgment for plaintiff" or "judgment for defendant," while an appellate court opinion will say "affirmed," "reversed," or "remanded" (which means the appellate court sent the case back to the trial court for further proceedings).

B. Other Features of a West Reporter

The West reporter volumes contain many helpful tables and reader's aids. Features found in current reporter volumes can include: Table of Cases Reported (alphabetical listing); Table of Cases Reported (by state or federal circuit); Statutes and Rules Tables; Standards for Criminal Justice Table; Words and Phrases Table; and Key Number Digest (for that reporter volume).

C. Federal Judicial Opinions

Unlike state court decisions, which are organized in West reporters by geographic region or state, federal court decisions are organized in reporters by the level of court.

1. United States Supreme Court

Decisions of the United States Supreme Court are available in print from several publishers. The official reporter is *United States Reports*. Unofficial reporters include West's *Supreme Court Reporter* and LexisNexis's *United States Supreme Court Reports, Lawyers' Edition*. In addition, opinions are available in *United States Law Week* ("USLW"), a weekly publication that often prints opinions before they appear in the advance sheets of the other print reporters.

United States Supreme Court decisions are available on the Court's own website, www.supremecourt.gov, and are typically submitted to the online commercial providers the same day the decisions are decided. Despite this availability, the Supreme Court maintains that only its print reporter, *United States Reports*, is official.

2. United States Courts of Appeals

Opinions of the United States Courts of Appeals are published in *Federal Reporter*, currently in its third series. All thirteen circuits' decisions are available in this print reporter.[10] In addition, each circuit maintains its own website and makes its decisions available there. Circuit court decisions are widely available from online commercial providers as well.

3. United States District Courts

Federal Supplement contains decisions from federal district courts. In addition, decisions that involve federal rules of civil procedure, evidence, and criminal procedure are published in *Federal Rules Decisions*. District court cases are also available online.

---

10. Selected decisions not published in the *Federal Reporter* series are published in the *Federal Appendix* reporter. These decisions are not treated as binding precedent by the courts.

D. Updating Reporters: Advance Sheets and Slip Opinions

Bound volumes of case reporters must be produced continually as new cases are heard and opinions are released for publication. Bound volumes of the various reporters are published as soon as there are enough cases from the corresponding jurisdiction (or group of jurisdictions) to fill a new volume. Between publication of these bound volumes, paper pamphlets called *advance sheets* are published. Some courts also publish individual *slip opinions* containing the court's opinion in one case.

1. Advance Sheets

Advance sheets are small, paperbound versions of reporters (like mini-reporters) published as often as weekly, depending on how soon a sufficient number of cases are collected to compile a new pamphlet. Advance sheets provide the text of recent court opinions, published in the same format and with the same pagination and citation as the opinions will have in the bound reporter volume (once it is published). Once a new bound volume is issued, the paperbound advance sheets are discarded by the library. Advance sheets for a given reporter series are located on the library shelves immediately following the most recent bound volume of the case reporters. The most recent copy on the shelf will probably be about three or four weeks old.

2. Slip Opinions

The most recent printed source of a case decision is a slip opinion. Each slip opinion contains only one case decision. Slip opinions are sent immediately to subscriber libraries and commercial online providers by the various clerks of court. Each slip opinion is available on that court's website. Indeed, some courts only issue slip opinions online.

Case opinions are available online in a variety of databases. Most courts have their own websites and usually post their decisions. Missouri court opinions are available online at www.courts.mo.gov. U.S. Supreme Court cases are available online at www.supremecourt.gov/opinions/opinions.aspx. Both WestlawNext and Lexis Advance contain numerous databases of case opinions, usually organized by jurisdiction or level of court.

Similar to a court's designation of its official print reporter, courts also designate whether the print or online publication is official. This becomes an issue only in the rare circumstance of a discrepancy between the opinion as it appears in print and as it appears online. The United States Supreme Court's position is that *United States Reports* is the official reporter of its opinions. The Missouri

Court of Appeals for the Western District maintains that the cases published on its website at www.courts.mo.gov are official. Indeed, the Missouri Court of Appeals for the Western District is one of the courts that no longer issues print slip opinions.

III. Digests

Reporters publish cases in rough chronological order, not by subject. A lawyer researching precedent related to a client's matter needs a way to search for opinions by subject. Digests serve this critical function.

A. West Digests

A *digest* is a topical index to case law reporters. West publishes separate digests for individual states, certain groups of states, certain groups of courts within the same jurisdiction, and all courts combined. *Missouri Digest 2d* is published by West.[11]

1. Headnotes

Digests are organized alphabetically in over 450 topics.[12] Under each topic is a series of paragraphs that are abstracts or short summaries of case opinions. Each abstract is referred to as a *headnote*, and a separate headnote is prepared for each unique point of law in each case opinion. These headnotes are identical to the headnotes in the cases as published in West reporters. Each headnote contains a succinct summary of the facts, law, or holding of the corresponding case as it relates to a certain point of law. The same headnotes may also appear in a West annotated code of statutes. Each headnote identifies the court that decided the case and the opinion's citation.

2. Topics and Key Numbers

Under each of the approximately 450 West digest topic headings are cases that deal with different subtopics. West assigns a key number to each subtopic.

---

11. Each of the West digests has had at least two series. The series are not cumulative, but cover different time periods, similar to the different series in reporters. The *Federal Practice Digest* has had four different series, which cover different time periods.

12. Each Descriptive-Word Index includes a Table of Abbreviations for all 450 plus topics.

A key number is a permanent, fixed number assigned by the West editorial staff to a specific point of law under a specific topic.

Every point of case law has its own topic and key number within the West digest and reporter systems. West uses the same topic and key number for a specific point of law throughout both the federal and state court systems and in every jurisdiction. It might help to think of the topic and key number system as an address. The topic is the street name, and the key number (referencing a point of law) is the house number. It would be difficult to find the specific house you were looking for with only the street name. You would have to start at the very beginning of the street and look at every house until you found the right one. However, if you have the house number and the street name, you can go straight to the right house.

Judicial opinions on WestlawNext will contain the topics and key numbers that may be on point with your issue. You can quickly move in a case from the headnote to the exact page where the point of law is discussed with one click. You can also move directly from the applicable topic and key number to another jurisdiction to locate additional authority.

3. Digest Sets

Cases can be "digested" or indexed in more than one print digest. A state court opinion may appear in a state digest, a regional digest (if available), and the *American/Decennial Digest*.[13] Cases from other jurisdictions that apply the same point of law will fall under the same topic and key number in those jurisdictions' digests. Thus, armed with the correct topic and key number, the legal researcher can unlock the door to cases from any jurisdiction dealing with a specific point of law.

B. Applying Research Approaches

The following pages explain how to research case decisions using the three approaches introduced in Chapter 1.

---

13. West's *American/Decennial Digest* is a digest series that encompasses all American jurisdictions, federal and state. Searching the *Decennial Digest* helps you avoid combing through each regional digest (and several state digests) to find each jurisdiction that has cases on your issue. The *Decennial Digest* is an invaluable resource when researching how several jurisdictions have decided an issue. The *Decennial Digest* can be quicker than an online search—it's much easier to scan through a page of headnotes than to scroll through each headnote one at a time online.

Table 3-1. Descriptive-Word Approach to Missouri Case Law Research

1. Generate a list of descriptive words.

2. Select a digest.

3. Search the Descriptive-Word Index of the digest to locate the descriptive words. Update this search by using the pocket parts of the index volumes.

4. Identify potentially applicable topics and key numbers.

5. Review the topics and key numbers in the digest volumes.

6. Identify potentially relevant cases from the headnotes in the digest volumes.

7. Update your topics and key numbers in the pocket parts, digest supplements, and the mini-digests of the reporters and advance sheets. Alternatively, update topics and key numbers on WestlawNext.

8. Read the cases in the reporters to determine their relevance.

1. Descriptive-Word Approach

Each set of West digests contains several volumes called the Descriptive-Word Index. The Descriptive-Word Index is a tool used to direct a researcher from descriptive words to the relevant topics and key numbers, which in turn lead to cases related to the problem or issue being researched. Table 3-1 summarizes this process. The Descriptive-Word Index contains thousands of entries, so it will likely have several entries that refer to your subject and will cross-reference the correct descriptive word used in the key number system.

a. Generating Descriptive Words

To begin the descriptive-word approach, identify the important facts or legal issues. Refer to Table 1-2 for examples in a burglary case.

b. Selecting a Digest

Next, decide which set of digests to consult, considering the jurisdiction whose law will ultimately resolve the issue. To consider the burglary example, you would look for Missouri case law. Two different digest sets index Missouri case law — *Missouri Digest* and the *American/Decennial Digest*.[14] *Missouri Digest*

---

14. West's regional reporter that includes Missouri judicial opinions, the *South Western Reporter*, does not have its own digest. Only four of the seven regional reporters have digests. Only the *Pacific Reporter*, *North Western Reporter*, *South Eastern Reporter*, and *Atlantic Reporter* have current digests. In the absence of a regional reporter digest,

serves as an index for the decisions of all reported Missouri state cases and cases of federal courts arising in or appealed from Missouri. As the narrowest digest, it will give the fewest extraneous cases. The second series of *Missouri Digest* contains the more recent Missouri cases.[15]

Next, select the volume of the Descriptive-Word Index from *Missouri Digest 2d* that covers the words that you selected from your list. Begin with the broadest word that is most closely related to the issue. For the burglary example, select the Descriptive-Word Index volume of *Missouri Digest 2d* that covers the word burglary and look it up. Note that the word burglary may have several subtopics listed beneath it. Next to each subtopic, in bold print, is the West topic and key number (or numbers) that leads you to cases dealing with that particular subtopic. Figure 3-4 illustrates a section of the Descriptive-Word Index listing under burglary.

Scan the entries for the subtopic Burglar's Tools. Find the digest topics and key numbers that apply. For example, Figure 3-4 shows that the elements of the crime of possession of burglar's tools are discussed at Burglary 12. Other topics and key numbers may also apply. You now have topics and key numbers to use in *Missouri Digest 2d* that cover burglar's tools.

Before leaving the Descriptive-Word Index, update your search by locating any pocket parts to the Descriptive-Word Index volumes you used.[16] If no pocket part exists, proceed to the digest's main volumes.

Select the digest volume covering topic and key number Burglary 12 to access case headnotes. Here you will see headnotes of Missouri cases where the courts have generally discussed possession of burglar's tools.

c. *Updating Your Search*

After checking the digest volume covering your topic and key number, update your search. The law might have changed since an older case or you might just want to use the most recent case to show that the law is still current.

---

researchers can either expand their research to the *American/Decennial Digest* or narrow their research to state-specific digests.

15. Do not shy away from the first series of any digest, however. Many rules of law set decades ago are still good law.

16. New words are constantly added to the Descriptive-Word Index because the law is constantly evolving. Thirty-five years ago, recognition of the disease AIDS was only beginning. As a result, the word "AIDS" did not appear in the Descriptive-Word Index. Now, it does.

Figure 3-4. *Missouri Digest 2d* **Descriptive-Word Index**

BURGLAR'S TOOLS

See heading **BURGLARY**, BURGLAR'S
   tools, possession of.

BURGLARY

ALARM systems, **Tel** ☞ 463

ATTEMPTS,
   Elements and requisites, **Burg** ☞ 11
   Pleading, **Burg** ☞ 26
   Sufficiency of evidence, **Burg** ☞ 41(10)

• • •

BURGLAR'S tools, possession of,
   Crime of,
   Elements and requisites, **Burg** ☞ 12
   Pleading, **Burg** ☞ 27
   Sufficiency of evidence, **Burg** ☞ 41(9)
   Evidence,
   Admissibility, **Burg** ☞ 37
   Sufficiency, crime of, **Burg** ☞ 41(9)
   Sufficiency, effect on, **Burg** ☞ 43

• • •

TOOLS. See subheading BURGLAR'S
   TOOLS under this heading.

Source: Missouri Digest 2d, Descriptive-Word Index, volume 44, pages 476–77, 480 (2001). Reprinted with permission of Thomson Reuters.

To update in print digests and reporters, check the pocket part to the topic volume, any supplemental pamphlet, and the "mini-digests" in the individual reporters and advance sheets to see whether more recent cases have been added to the digest under your key number since the digest volume was published. At the beginning of each digest main volume, pocket part, and supplement is a table that states the coverage of that issue. This coverage table gives the volume number of the last reporter digested in that issue. A researcher then knows in which reporter volume to begin looking at the mini-digest. Look in each reporter and advance sheet volume's mini-digest published after the volume number in the coverage table.

d. Finding More Topics and Key Numbers

Utilizing this same basic method of research, you can find the appropriate West topic and key number for any of the words or phrases from your research problem. Remember that any number of descriptive words may lead to the same topic and key number and that more than one topic and key number may lead to relevant cases. If you are having difficulty finding an appropriate topic by using your initial descriptive words, try to think of other descriptive words, synonyms, or closely related words that correspond to the circumstances of your case.

Armed with the correct topic and key number, you can expand your search to any digest set within the West Reporting System to find additional case law on point. Thus, if you want cases from Illinois that discuss possession of burglar's tools, you need only go to the appropriate volume of *Illinois Digest 2d* and look under Burglary 12.

e. Using the Descriptive-Word Approach in Online Sources
i. Using Search Queries

You could use the descriptive-word approach in either Lexis Advance or WestlawNext to construct a search query using descriptive words to search the full text of cases in any of several databases containing Missouri cases. Constructing a search query is discussed in Chapter 8. Try to use the narrowest database possible, just as you try to use the narrowest digest possible. Using the narrowest database usually has a lower cost than a more expansive database.

ii. Using Topics and Key Numbers in Online Sources

Topics and key numbers are a feature of West and are only available on West-lawNext. You can search using a topic and key number to find additional authority directly through the key numbers feature on WestlawNext. This feature operates like a print case digest, but there is no need to search through pocket parts and mini-digests! WestlawNext has gathered all relevant information in one list for you in a customized digest. Note that WestlawNext converts the topic and key number into one number that includes the letter "k." The k stands for "key number." WestlawNext assigns a number to each topic, which appears first. After the k is the same number used in the topic and key number in the print digests. In WestlawNext, the topics and key numbers are displayed in a graphical outline.

Lexis Advance has its own system of topics and key numbers. When you click on your desired subtopic, a drop-down box appears. Click "Get documents" and you will be sent to the additional authority on your topic. To assist you in constructing your search query, Lexis Advance includes a "Core Terms" section near the top of each case authority. This section lists other possible search words to use. Figure 3-5 illustrates this feature.

Figure 3-5. Core Terms in Lexis Advance

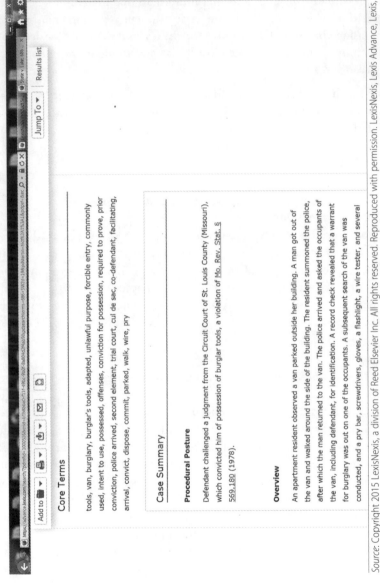

Core Terms

tools, van, burglary, burglar's tools, adapted, unlawful purpose, forcible entry, commonly used, intent to use, possessed, offenses, conviction for possession, required to prove, prior conviction, police arrived, second element, trial court, cul de sac, co-defendant, facilitating, arrival, convict, dispose, commit, parked, walk, wire, pry

Case Summary

Procedural Posture

Defendant challenged a judgment from the Circuit Court of St. Louis County (Missouri), which convicted him of possession of burglar tools, a violation of Mo. Rev. Stat. § 569.180 (1978).

Overview

An apartment resident observed a van parked outside her building. A man got out of the van and walked around the side of the building. The resident summoned the police, after which the man returned to the van. The police arrived and asked the occupants of the van, including defendant, for identification. A record check revealed that a warrant for burglary was out on one of the occupants. A subsequent search of the van was conducted, and a pry bar, screwdrivers, gloves, a flashlight, a wire tester, and several

2. Known-Topic Approach

If you are familiar with the applicable area of law, rather than first looking in the Descriptive-Word Index volume(s), go immediately to the topic volume in the set of digests covering the applicable jurisdiction. For example, since

Figure 3-6. *Missouri Digest 2d* **Topic Outline**

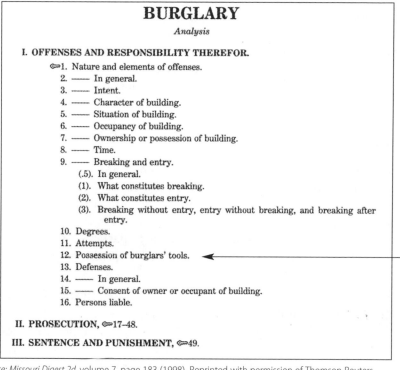

Source: *Missouri Digest 2d*, volume 7, page 183 (1998). Reprinted with permission of Thomson Reuters.

you now know that the West digest system has a topic called Burglary, rather than looking up burglary or tools in the Descriptive-Word Index, you could proceed directly to the volume of the digest covering burglary. At the beginning of each topic in the digests, West provides a very detailed topic outline that begins with a general summary of major subtopics, followed by a listing of all individual key numbers that apply to those subtopics. Figure 3-6 is an excerpt of the analysis outline for the topic burglary. By glancing through the topic outline, you can find a subtopic that narrowly focuses on your research issue, and directly before that subtopic description will be the key number that applies to that subtopic.

The next step is the same as in the descriptive-word approach — scanning through the headnotes to find those relating to the specific key number that is on point. Following the key number are headnotes of cases discussing that narrow subtopic.

Remember to be sure to update by checking the pocket part of the topic volume of the digest, any supplemental digest pamphlet, and any mini-digests in the reporters and advance sheets published later than the digest's pocket part or supplemental pamphlet for additional cases under your topic and key number. Alternatively, check the topic and key number online for more recent cases. Again, the same topic and key number can be used throughout the West digest system to find additional cases from other jurisdictions.

Both Lexis Advance and WestlawNext provide features that allow a researcher who already knows the specific topic to perhaps move more quickly to find relevant authority.

Searching by topic is available on Lexis Advance through the "Browse" feature. Click on "Browse" at the top of the page on the left. You then have a choice of "Sources" or "Topics." Click on "Topics." You are then given a list of topics. After clicking on a topic, you are then given a list of subtopics. Clicking on a subtopic may lead to more subtopics or to particular statutes. Thus, searching by this feature can limit the scope of your research to focus on a smaller range of authority.

In WestlawNext, the known-topic approach works through West's key numbers feature. On the opening screen, the link to the digest includes a symbol shaped like a key and the title "Key Numbers." When you click on the link, the index to the digest topics appears. This screen allows you to choose the jurisdiction you wish to search. You can then click on the relevant topic directly to see the complete list of key numbers for that topic. You can then locate potentially relevant key numbers and authorities through perusing the index of key numbers for that topic or by entering descriptive words in the search box.

The key numbers feature allows you to narrow your search from broad to narrow topics. As an example, to research the liability of a corporation to clean up a polluted lake, click on the topic "Insurance," then subtopics "Coverage — Health and Accident Insurance" and then "Mandatory coverage." Select the jurisdiction. You will see the same list you would have seen in the print digest. You can then use the "Search within results" feature to narrow the search.

You can also search WestlawNext using topics without key numbers by browsing "Practice Areas." On the main screen, click on the tab marked "Practice Areas" and you will find a list of topics. After clicking on a topic, you are sent to a page including current news on the topic and a list of authority. That list limits the authority to those on your topic.

3. Known-Authority Approach

a. WestlawNext

If you already have one case dealing with the issue or area of law that applies to your research problem, skip both the Descriptive-Word Index and the digest topic outline—the appropriate topic and key number is already available to you in the headnotes of the known case. If you already have a copy of a known case, scroll through the beginning of the case until you reach the numbered headnotes of the case opinion and find the headnote that most closely addresses the issue or point of law that you are researching. Immediately following the headnote number, you will find the West topic and key number assigned to that specific point of law. With the topic and key number from the headnote, you can proceed directly to the appropriate jurisdictional digest volume covering that topic. Remember to click on the topic and key number and not the headnote number instead. The headnote number will jump to the place in that same case where that part of law is discussed. In WestlawNext, click on the subtopic, and you will be sent directly to the list of authorities for your default jurisdiction.

While an opinion's headnotes lead you to topics and key numbers on your issue, the opinion itself will cite to other authority that may be helpful. This authority could include other court opinions, statutes, and secondary sources. When you have known authority on point, you can also use citators to find other authority as discussed in Chapter 5.

b. Lexis Advance

Similar to WestlawNext, you can use the headnotes in Lexis Advance to locate additional authority. In addition, a unique feature of Lexis Advance helps you locate additional authority. It is accessible through the known-authority approach. "Activate Passages" allows a researcher to locate more similar authority or authority with similar language. This feature relies on a computer program rather than a legal analyst to decide which cases and language are similar to those selected. Thus, your results depend on how closely the program matches your authority with others.

c. Narrowing Your Results Online

Both WestlawNext and Lexis Advance allow a researcher to construct a search within the document itself. "Search Text" on WestlawNext (Figure 3-7) and "Search Within Results" and "Jump to" on Lexis Advance search the found document for specific terms. Thus, a researcher can quickly find every place in the document where a specific term is used. Even better, each service is free. No extra charges are incurred to locate terms within the search.

Figure 3-7. Search Text on WestlawNext

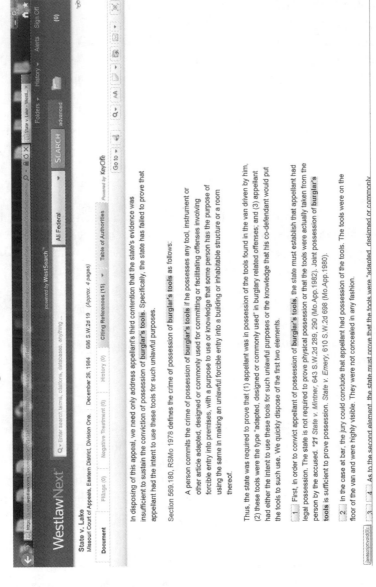

Source: WestlawNext. Reprinted with permission of Thomson Reuters.

Just as in print resources, already knowing even one applicable authority unlocks the door to the entire interlocking system of legal authority. The difference with computer-assisted legal research is that hyperlinks and other features of the computer are highly efficient in moving between sources.

C. Additional Research Aids in a Digest

In addition to the Descriptive-Word Index and the alphabetically arranged topic volumes, each jurisdictional digest set contains Table of Cases volumes. These volumes are located at the end of the digest series. The Table of Cases volumes list all cases for the corresponding digest alphabetically by party names. If you know the name of the plaintiff or the defendant in a case, but not the complete case citation, you can refer to the Table of Cases volumes to find the full citation. There are also pocket part updates, supplemental pamphlets, and bound supplements for the Table of Cases volumes. Note that for digests with more than one series, each series has its own Table of Cases volumes for the period covered by that series. For example, there is a separate Table of Cases for *Federal Practice Digest, Third* and for *Federal Practice Digest, Fourth*. You can also use a party's name as a search term on both Lexis Advance and WestlawNext.

Each digest set also has a Words and Phrases volume. This volume shows whether a court has given certain words a legal definition. The Words and Phrases volume shows this by directing the researcher to a case that defines the word for that jurisdiction. West includes the topic and key number used in that case. Words and Phrases volumes are particularly helpful when a statutory term is vague. Like the Table of Cases, Words and Phrases is updated through pocket parts and supplemental pamphlets.

IV. Summary

Judicial opinions form the bedrock of American jurisprudence. Case reporters compile judicial opinions in an essentially chronological manner. A legal researcher who already knows the citation of relevant authority can go directly to the case reporter or online database to locate the opinion. Most of the time, however, the researcher does not have a citation and needs to locate authority.

Although researching case law in the digest system is a very effective method of finding primary authority, this method has several pitfalls for the unwary researcher. First, the digests contain only headnotes of issues or rules of law addressed by cases in the corresponding jurisdiction, rather than the actual court opinions. Thus, the researcher must never rely on these headnote summaries as primary authority. Rather, the headnote should lead the researcher to the case opinion, published in a print reporter or available online, which can then be read and analyzed for its primary authority value in a research problem.

As a researcher you must realize West editors choose the digest classifications and subdivide the text of the case opinions into the various topics and key numbers. You must use your own analysis and judgment regarding the court's holding and opinion. By keeping these two caveats in mind, you can take advantage of the vast benefits that digests provide.

Chapter 4

Administrative Law

Administrative law is a complex body of executive orders, agency regulations, and agency decisions. This law is issued by the Governor or the President, by the various departments within the executive branch of the state or federal government, and by the numerous independent administrative agencies created by a state legislature or Congress.

Administrative agencies make law in two ways: rulemaking and adjudication. *Rulemaking* is the quasi-legislative function of an agency. Using powers that have been delegated to it by a state legislature or Congress through a particular statute,[1] each agency promulgates rules or regulations[2] to carry out specific legislative purposes. For example, the Endangered Species Act, 16 U.S.C. § 1533(d), provides that the Secretary of the Interior shall issue such regulations as deemed necessary to provide for the conservation of threatened or endangered species. A division of the Department of the Interior, the U.S. Fish and Wildlife Service, then drafts and publishes rules that implement that legislative directive. These rules are written in a format similar to statutes, though administrative rules are often more specific than statutes.

The second form of administrative lawmaking is *adjudication.* Adjudication is the quasi-judicial power of agencies to render decisions in cases arising under statutory and regulatory law. For example, under Missouri Employment Security Law, anyone denied unemployment benefits may file a written protest of the agency's determination within ten days.[3] The director of the Division of Employment Security under the Department of Labor and Industrial Re-

---

1. A statute that delegates power to an administrative agency is called the "enabling statute."
2. The terms "rules" and "regulations" have identical meanings. *See The Federal Register: What It Is and How to Use It* 33 (Robert D. Fox & Ernie Sowada eds., 1985).
3. § 288.070(1) RSMo Supp. 2013.

lations is required "to designate an impartial referee or referees to hear and decide disputed determinations" and claims.[4]

In Missouri, agency hearings are conducted by a hearing officer, referee, or administrative law judge (ALJ). Federal law hearings are conducted by an ALJ. Agency hearings are then subject to review both within the agency and in state or federal court. Indeed, a litigant must first exhaust all administrative remedies before proceeding to judicial review in court. Missouri Administrative Procedures and Review statutes[5] created the Administrative Hearing Commission (AHC),[6] which has two functions. First, the AHC conducts some initial hearings for certain agencies pursuant to statute. Second, it operates as the first step of review after some, but not all, agencies make their final determination. Following AHC review, the parties may seek judicial review in the courts.

I. Missouri Administrative Rulemaking

For a thorough overview of Missouri administrative law, use the red, two-volume *Missouri Administrative Law* published by The Missouri Bar. It includes an overview of all the departments and agencies in Missouri. If you are unfamiliar with a particular Missouri agency, this book would be a good place to get an overview of its responsibilities.

A. Resources

Administrative rulemaking documents are found in two primary places. The first, the *Missouri Register*, is a daily compilation of agency action. The *Missouri Register* is arranged chronologically. The second resource for administrative rulemaking documents is the *Code of State Regulations* (CSR). This is an annual codification by subject of the permanent rules published in the *Missouri Register*.

The *Missouri Register* has been published since May 1976. It was published monthly from 1976 to 1986 and has been published semi-monthly since then. Each issue contains a variety of documents.

- **Emergency rules**—An agency issues emergency rules when the agency finds that an immediate danger to the public health, safety, or welfare

---

4. §288.190(1) RSMo Supp. 2013.

5. §536.010 *et seq.* RSMo.

6. §621.015 *et seq.* RSMo; *see also* Mo. Code Regs. Ann. tit. 1, §15-3.200 *et seq.* (2011).

exists or a compelling governmental interest requires emergency action. These are typically the first documents in the *Missouri Register*.

- **Executive orders**—The Governor, as the chief executive for Missouri, has the power to issue these orders under Missouri's constitution and by statute.

- **Proposed rules**—Each agency publishes proposed rules and changes to existing rules in the *Missouri Register*. This publication constitutes notice to the general public.

- **Orders of rulemaking**—The *Missouri Register* publishes final rules as issued by the agency.

- **Dissolutions**—Notices of the dissolution of limited liability companies and limited partnerships are included in the back of each *Missouri Register*.

In addition, each issue of the *Missouri Register* includes research aids called "Source Guides." The "Rule Changes Since Last Update to Code of State Regulations" table includes all emergency, proposed, and final rules issued since the last update to CSR. The "Emergency Rules" table lists all emergency rules currently in effect. The "Executive Orders" table catalogs all current governor's orders. The "Index" is a topical index to the *Missouri Register* that includes both the rule number and the *Missouri Register* publication date.

The *Code of State Regulations* (CSR) is the topical compilation of Missouri administrative regulations. The CSR currently consists of twenty-two titles, which are housed in fifteen red notebooks. Each title corresponds to a Missouri administrative agency. The CSR has a general index, published by the state, organized by subject and department. It includes tables that cross-reference Missouri statutes. The index is in volume fifteen.

The Missouri Secretary of State's website has links to the *Missouri Register*, www.sos.mo.gov/adrules/morcg/moreg.asp; to the CSR, www.sos.mo.gov/adrules/csr/csr.asp; and to executive orders, www.sos.mo.gov/library/reference/orders/default.asp. Both WestlawNext and Lexis Advance include the CSR in their Missouri databases. While Lexis Advance also includes the *Missouri Register* as a separate database, WestlawNext features another database, "Missouri Regulations Tracking," that keeps a researcher apprised of proposed rules and other features found in the *Missouri Register*.

Figure 4-1. *Code of State Regulations* General Index

CHILD SUPPORT ENFORCEMENT
claims submissions; 13 CSR 30-3.020
credit reporting; 13 CSR 30-6.010
financial performance measures; 13 CSR 30-2.020
hearings, administrative; 13 CSR 30-7.010
incentives; 13 CSR 30-9.010
income withholding
    exceptions; 13 CSR 30-4.020
    procedures; 13 CSR 30-4.010
IV-D child support payments
    collection; 13 CSR 30-2.030, 13 CSR 30-2.040
    distribution; 13 CSR 30-2.030, 13 CSR 30-2.040
organization; 13 CSR 30-1.010
performance standards, prosecuting attorney; 13 CSR 30-2.010
public assistance recipients, cooperation requirement; 13 CSR 30-8.010
record keeping, requirements; 13 CSR 30-3.020
reimbursement; 13 CSR 30-3.010
review, modifications, child support orders; 13 CSR 30-5.020

Source: Code of State Regulations, General Index, volume 15, page 13 (2014).

B. Researching Missouri Administrative Regulations

1. Descriptive-Word Approach

To begin using the CSR, make a list of descriptive words and look them up in the index. Note that the index is centered more on the agencies themselves rather than words that lead you to rules. Thus, your list of descriptive words should include the name of the agency. The index will refer to a specific regulation. Turn to that regulation, and read its text carefully. Update the regulation by reviewing the latest cumulative issue of the *Missouri Register* published since the CSR online or in print. Update the enabling statute by referring to the "Authority" note following the regulation and using the strategies for updating statutes described in Chapter 2 of this book.

The excerpts in Figures 4-1 through 4-4 and Table 4-1 illustrate CSR research in a child support case. Assume your client is concerned that being one week late on his child support payment will be reported to credit reporting agencies. You know that the Missouri Department of Social Services has a division dedicated to child support enforcement. You decide to research Missouri regulations to see when non-payment of child support is reported to credit reporting agencies.

Begin with the General Index of CSR, as shown in Figure 4-1. The index topic "child support enforcement" has a subtopic "credit reporting" that refers to 13 CSR 30-6.010. Title 13 of CSR includes all regulations of the Department of Social Services. Division 30 governs child support enforcement. The number 6.010 references a specific regulation issued by this agency.

Each regulation begins with a statement of its purpose, as illustrated in Figure 4-2. Figure 4-3 shows the applicable subsection of 13 CSR § 30-6.010. According to this regulation, your client's late payment will not be reported unless it is two months late with an arrearage (past due amount) of at least $1,000.[7]

At the end of each regulation is an authority note that lists the enabling statute, including any prior amendments. Figure 4-4 is the authority note for 13 CSR 30-6.010; the enabling statute for that regulation is 454.400 RSMo 1994. Always check the enabling statute to see whether the rule exceeds the agency's power or jurisdiction. To update the enabling statute, check pocket parts and *Vernon's Missouri Legislative Service*, as described in Chapter 2.

Figure 4-2. 13 CSR § 30.6010 Purpose

**Title 13—DEPARTMENT OF
SOCIAL SERVICES**
Division 30—Child Support Enforcement
Chapter 6—Credit Reporting

13 CSR 30-6.010 Reporting of Child Support Debts to Consumer Reporting Agencies

PURPOSE: The purpose of this rule is to establish procedures where a consumer reporting agency may request debt information from the Division of Child Support Enforcement (DCSE). It also contains procedures for DCSE to report an absent parent who has an arrearage of $1000 or more to consumer reporting agencies. This rule references 13 CSR 30-7.010, regarding procedures where an absent parent, whose debt is to be reported to a consumer reporting agency, may request and receive an administrative hearing regarding the report. The information given to consumer reporting agencies will be used to update individual consumer records.

Source: Code of State Regulations, volume 9, Department of Social Services, chapter 6, page 3 (2001).

---

7. Under Mo. Code Regs. Ann. tit. 13, § 30-6.010(1), a "consumer reporting agency" includes a credit bureau.

Figure 4-3. 13 CSR § 30.6010(2)(A)(1) Text

(2) Division (IV-D) Responsibilities.
(A) If a noncustodial parent.
1. Is at least two (2) months delinquent in the payment of support and the arrearage is one thousand dollars ($1,000) or more, the division shall periodically report to consumer reporting agencies a noncustodial parent's name and other identifying information specified in subsection (2)(D) and may continue to do so after the arrearage is less than one thousand dollars ($1000) . . . .

Source: Code of State Regulations, volume 9, Department of Social Services, chapter 6, page 3 (2001).

Figure 4-4. 13 CSR § 30.6010 Authority

AUTHORITY: section 454.400, RSMo 1994.* Original rule filed Dec. 13, 1989, effective April 26, 1990. Emergency amendment filed June 2, 1995, effective July 15, 1995, expired Nov. 11, 1995. Amended: Filed June 2, 1995, effective Sept. 30, 1995.

*Original authority: 454.400, RSMo 1982, amended 1985, 1986, 1990, 1993.

Source: Code of State Regulations, volume 9, Department of Social Services, chapter 6, page 3 (2001).

2. Known-Topic Approach

Because each title of CSR consists of a single Missouri agency, once a researcher knows which agency likely promulgates rules on the topic, the researcher can use the known-topic approach. At the beginning of each title is an outline organized by the divisions within the agency. At the beginning of each chapter of each division is an outline of the specific rules for that chapter. Using the known-topic approach requires a researcher to check the title outline to determine the appropriate division and then to check the chapter outline for the specific topic.

3. Known-Authority Approach

Much of the time, a researcher learns about an applicable state regulation from a secondary source, such as Missouri CLE Deskbooks, discussed in Chapter 6 of this book. A researcher can also discover relevant regulations from the annotations following an enabling statute that includes citations to the promulgated regulations.

C. Updating the Language of an Administrative Rule

To update the rule itself, look at the latest cumulative issue of the *Missouri Register* issued since the latest publication of the CSR. The "Rule Changes Since Last Update to Code of State Regulations" table is a cumulative table of changes to CSR sections since the last update of CSR. Table 4-1 is an excerpt from the March 2, 2015, table.

Table 4-1. Excerpt from *Missouri Register*
Rule Changes Since Update to Code of State Regulations

Rule Number	Agency	Emergency	Proposed	Order
	Department of Labor And Industrial Relations			
8 CSR 30-3.060	Divisions of Labor Standards		39 MoReg 211	39 MoReg 2133
	Department of Natural Resources			
10 CSR 10-6.110	Air Conservation Commission		39 MoReg 1509	40 MoReg 138
10 CSR 100-5.010	Petroleum Storage Tank Insurance Fund Board of Trustees		39 MoReg 1443	40 MoReg 193
10 CSR 100-6.010			39 MoReg 1445	40 MoReg 194

Source: Missouri Register, volume 40, number 5 (Mar. 2, 2015).

D. Online Sources

Missouri administrative agencies have websites to make information about agency rules, proposed rules, and procedures more readily available to the public. To learn the web address for the applicable Missouri agency, search www.mo.gov. A drop-down menu is provided for "Government." The "Executive Branch" link provides an alphabetical listing of agencies and includes hyperlinks to send you directly to each agency's website. Each Missouri administrative agency website is organized and set up differently. These websites are designed for consumers, not legal researchers. Thus, you'll usually need to delve a bit to be able to search for rules and proposed rules directly.

Both Lexis Advance and WestlawNext provide access to Missouri administrative law. Lexis Advance includes the *Missouri Register* as a database, while WestlawNext provides an alternative, "Missouri Regulation Tracking." A researcher could also use these online services to find the language of a Missouri rule. Lexis Advance maintains the "Missouri Code of State Regulations" database, while WestlawNext maintains the "Missouri Regulations" database. In addition, WestlawNext has a separate database for "Historical Regulations."

II. Missouri Administrative Adjudication

An administrative agency holds hearings on issues or complaints brought under its jurisdiction as determined by its enabling legislation. These hearings are overseen by a hearing officer, referee, or administrative law judge (ALJ). These decisions are not readily available.

Appeals from some agencies' decisions are heard by the Administrative Hearing Commission (AHC). In addition, an agency or individual can begin a complaint with the commission itself when the AHC has jurisdiction over the matter as specified by statute. The AHC makes decisions under a contested case procedure, similar to a trial. Besides this jurisdiction, the AHC also contracts with other state agencies to conduct initial proceedings and make a recommendation to that agency.

Decisions of the AHC are available in print at the Missouri Supreme Court Library. The decisions are also available online on the AHC's website at www.ahc.mo.gov. AHC decisions are searchable by case number or by the board or commission's name. The website contains information on the AHC's procedures, the forms needed, and a jurisdiction chart of various agency boards and commissions. Some AHC and other agency decisions are also available on WestlawNext and Lexis Advance.[8]

III. Federal Administrative Law

Federal administrative law research is similar to Missouri administrative law research. Rulemaking documents are available both in a chronological compilation called the *Federal Register* and in a codified form called the *Code of Federal Regulations* (CFR).

There are two types of federal agencies: independent agencies and executive agencies. An *independent* regulatory agency is an agency whose officials are appointed by the President and approved by the Senate for a fixed term of years. The fixed term is intended to insulate the agency and its officials from the politics of the President or Congress. Examples of federal independent agencies include the Central Intelligence Agency, the Environmental Protection Agency, the Federal Communications Commission, the Federal Trade Commission, and the United States Postal Service. *Executive* agencies, on the other hand, are agencies whose officials are appointed by the President and can be removed at any time by the President. Thus, the officials of the executive agencies change with each new President. Examples of executive agencies include the Department of State, the Department of Justice, and the Department of Defense.

A. Federal Administrative Rulemaking

1. *Federal Register*

The *Federal Register* is published every federal governmental working day and contains the notices, rules, and regulations promulgated that day by the President or an administrative agency. The *Federal Register* provides official notice to the public of new administrative regulations. Some of these notices are not available anywhere else. New regulations issued in the *Federal Register* can be used as prima facie evidence in courts as a true copy of an original administrative document.

---

8. Administrative law decisions have less precedential value than court decisions because most of the agencies do not strictly adhere to the doctrine of *stare decisis* and therefore do not feel absolutely bound to follow their own previous decisions in a later case. *State ex rel. Praxair v. Public Serv. Comm'n*, 328 S.W.3d 329, 340 (Mo. App. W.D. 2010). Attorneys must still know the status of particular decisions when practicing before an agency or appealing an agency decision.

The pages in the *Federal Register* are numbered chronologically, beginning with page 1 in January of each year. Law libraries may have copies of the *Federal Register* in print or on microfiche. The latest shelf issue is generally one week out-of-date, while the microfiche has a lag time of about two months.

More recent *Federal Register* information can be accessed online. Both Lexis Advance and WestlawNext have the *Federal Register* online from July 1980 to within two to four days of publication. For free online access to the *Federal Register*, go to www.gpo.gov/fdsys/browse/collection.action?collectionCode=FR. In addition, agencies often post proposed rules and their specific title of CFR on their websites in either a "Reading Room" or "Resources" link. A list of all agency websites is available at www.loc.gov/rr/news/fedgov.html and at www.regulations.gov/#!home. You can search for any federal agency or search for relevant regulations by keyword.

Therefore, if you were looking for an agency rule or regulation that you knew was promulgated on a certain date two weeks ago, you could go to the shelf and look at a hard copy of the rule, or you could search online. If the rule was promulgated the day before yesterday, a computer research service or the Internet would be the best bet.

Congress requires that certain information be included in the daily *Federal Register*:

- **Table of Contents ("Contents")** — The documents in the Contents are arranged alphabetically by the agency that created them.
- **CFR Parts Affected in this Issue** — This table lists all CFR parts that have been modified by a document in the *Federal Register* volume. It is usually directly after the Contents.
- **Presidential Documents** — Not all *Federal Register* volumes will contain presidential documents. If there are any in the issue, they will be listed in the Contents under "Presidential documents." Normally, presidential documents will be the first documents contained in a volume of the *Federal Register*.
- **Rules and Regulations** — The type of document (e.g., rule, proposed rule, notice) is identified on the top right-hand corner of each page. Each document contains a heading that lists the name of the agency, the CFR title and part affected (i.e., where the rule will eventually be codified by topic in the CFR), a brief description of the subject of the document, and the type of action. The body of the document contains the summary section, the effective date, and a name and address of someone to contact for further information. The actual amendment usually appears at the end of the entry.

- **Proposed Rules**—"A proposed rule document is an announcement to the public that a change to the CFR is being considered."[9] The format is generally the same as for final rules. The date listed, however, is the deadline for submission of comments rather than the effective date. The address is given for submission of comments.
- **Notices**—"This section contains documents other than rules and proposed rules that are applicable to the public."[10] Notices are not codified in the CFR; thus, the *Federal Register* is the only place you can access a copy of a notice.
- **Sunshine Act Meetings**—The "Sunshine Act"[11] requires that meetings of government agencies be open to the public and that public announcements of the time and place of the meeting must be made in the *Federal Register*. This publication is also the notice function of the *Federal Register*.

Each volume of the *Federal Register* also lists valuable information in a section called "Reader Aids." This section includes phone numbers for information and assistance; a listing of *Federal Register* pages and dates for the month of which this volume is a part; a cumulative list of CFR parts affected during that month; a list of rules going into effect on that day; and a list of public laws enacted during that session of Congress.

Critically important is the "CFR Parts Affected" table located at the very end of the issue. This expanded section includes all CFR parts affected during that month. This listing provides a tool to update a whole month at one time without having to look at each daily *Federal Register*. This feature is found in all *Federal Register* issues. The use of this feature will become clearer in the subsequent discussion of the *Code of Federal Regulations*.

2. *Federal Register Index*

Because the *Federal Register* is organized chronologically by date, you will most often need to consult the *Federal Register Index* to guide you to the appropriate volume of the *Federal Register*. Only one index to the *Federal Register* is available—the official *Federal Register Index* published by the federal government. The official *Federal Register Index* is a separate government publication from the *Federal Register* and is issued monthly in cumulative form.

---

9. Fox & Sowada, *supra* note 2, at 59.
10. *Id.* at 49.
11. 5 U.S.C. § 552b (2012).

3. *Code of Federal Regulations*

The *Code of Federal Regulations* (CFR) is a codification by subject of all federal regulations. The CFR includes all regulations currently in effect no matter when they appeared in the *Federal Register*. The fifty titles of the CFR correspond roughly to the fifty-two titles of the United States Code (U.S.C.). For example, Title 7 is Agriculture both in the U.S.C. and in the CFR. Not all titles correspond directly. Title 40 of the CFR, for example, is Protection of the Environment, while Title 40 of the U.S.C. is Public Buildings, Property, and Works.

Each of the fifty titles of the CFR is divided into chapters, parts, and sections. Each chapter is concerned with a specific agency, each part contains the regulations on a certain topic, and each section covers one regulation. For example, 40 CFR § 52.1320 is:

> Title 40 (Protection of Environment)
> > Chapter I (Environmental Protection Agency)
> > > Part 52 (Approval and Promulgation of Implementation Plans)
> > > > Section 1320 (Missouri)

Note that the citation to a particular regulation includes the title and a combined number indicating the part and section.

Right before the text of the part, an "authority" note provides the statutory or executive authority under which the regulation was issued. Following the authority note is a "source" note giving the *Federal Register* citations and date where the part was last published there in full.

The CFR contains the current text of agency regulations as of the date printed on the volume cover. The CFR is updated each year on a revolving, quarterly basis. This revolving updating system is immediately apparent because some of the book covers are different colors. The different colored paper jackets reflect this revolving, piecemeal updating. Titles 1–16, for example, are updated as of January 1 each year; Titles 17–27 are updated as of April 1; Titles 28–41 as of July 1; and Titles 42–50 as of October 1.

The CFR can also be found on microfiche from 1938 forward. In addition, the CFR versions since 1984 are also available on both Lexis Nexis and Westlaw. You can also find the current version of CFR on the Internet at no cost at www.gpo.gov/fdsys/browse/collectionCfr.action?collectionCode=CFR. Each individual agency's website will also have links to the relevant titles of CFR.

4. CFR Research

All three research approaches introduced in Chapter 1 can be used with administrative law. The descriptive-word approach operates through the *CFR Index and Finding Aids*, a separate government publication printed by the Government Printing Office. The *CFR Index and Finding Aids* is arranged by subject matter and is revised once a year. A flow chart of this approach is provided in Table 4-2.

Each title of CFR begins with an outline, and you can use the known-topic approach by perusing this outline. It may be more efficient to use the individual agency's website to help pare down the rules you need to peruse when you already know the name of the agency.

If you have a citation to a regulation, you can use the known-authority approach and proceed directly to the applicable CFR section. The known-authority approach can also be used if you know the enabling statute's citation rather than the CFR citation. You can quickly locate regulations that have been promulgated under its statutory authority by using Table 1 of the *CFR Index and Finding Aids*, "Parallel Table of Authorities and Rules." This table lists every statute and presidential document cited as authority for a particular regulation in the CFR. Similarly, U.S.C.S. contains a "reverse" table, which gives appropriate U.S.C. citations when you know the CFR cite, in its "Index and Finding Aids to Code of Federal Regulations." In addition, the appropriate CFR citation is in the "Library References" of U.S.C.A. or following the U.S.C.S. version of the statute.

Another approach to finding regulations currently in force is to use one of the myriad of looseleaf services for the particular area of law that you are researching. These services collect the relevant federal agency rulemaking information and can often eliminate the need for much of the work involved in finding and updating the federal regulatory scheme. Looseleafs are discussed in Chapter 6.

5. Updating the CFR

The regulations on the agency websites and on Lexis Advance and West-lawNext usually are more current than the print version. But looking online is not the end of updating an administrative regulation. Attorneys practicing in a regulatory field must keep track of proposed administrative rules as well. Clients routinely need advice regarding proposed rules that may affect their business. Proposed rules are located only in the *Federal Register*. To locate proposed rules efficiently and at no cost, go to the website of the agency that promulgated the rule and you will be linked to that proposed rule in the *Federal*

**Table 4-2. Descriptive-Word Approach to
Federal Administrative Law Research**

1. Generate a list of descriptive words.
2. In print, go to the *CFR Index & Finding Aids* volume. When searching online, go to the agency's website, if known. If you do not know the relevant agency, use a commercial provider's service and select a source that includes CFR.
3. Search the index for the descriptive words in print or run a search with your descriptive words in the online search engine for the service you selected.
4. Identify applicable code sections.
5. Locate code sections in the appropriate volume of the print CFR or click on the code section online.
6. Read the potentially relevant code sections and surrounding sections to determine the preliminary answer to question.
7. Review the outline of sections for that title for other possible code sections.
8. Update the code sections through the *Federal Register*.

Register. You could also access a WestlawNext or Lexis Advance database that contains the *Federal Register* to locate proposed rules.

After updating CFR to be sure you have the most current language of the rule, check for judicial treatment of a section of the CFR by using a citator. Citators are discussed in depth in Chapter 5.

6. Presidential Documents

Presidential executive orders, proclamations, and other documents are issued pursuant to either specific statutory authority or inherent executive powers granted by the Constitution. Executive orders cover a wide range of issues and are generally made effective upon publication in the *Federal Register*. Presidential documents are assigned permanent identifying numbers and are listed separately in the *Federal Register*. Each year, these documents are compiled into Title 3 of the CFR. Chapter 1 of Title 3 is a codification of current regulations governing the executive branch itself. Despite its inclusion within the CFR, Title 3 is not part of the CFR codification. It is simply a compilation of all presidential documents created in that year. Documents that have been amended or repealed remain in the compilation.

A separate, chronological source for presidential documents since 1965 is the government-published *Weekly Compilation of Presidential Documents*. Each issue contains its own index. The latest copies are also available at www.gpo.gov/fdsys/browse/collection.action?collectionCode=CPD. A companion publication is the *Public Papers of the Presidents*, also available online at www.gpo.gov/fdsys/browse/collection.action?collectionCode=PPP. Online, Lexis Advance has all presidential documents since January 1981; WestlawNext has executive orders back to 1936 and other documents since 1984.

B. Federal Administrative Adjudication

Nearly all federal administrative agencies are delegated quasi-judicial power to rule on cases and controversies arising under their enabling statute or their own regulatory law. This adjudication function is the second way in which administrative agencies make law.

Administrative law judges within most regulatory agencies, like federal judges appointed under Article III of the Constitution, issue formal written opinions that are later published in official agency reporters. These reporters are different from the case reporters covered in Chapter 3. By way of example, the *FCC Record* is the official reporter for the Federal Communications Commission, an independent regulatory agency. The *FCC Record* publishes administrative decisions issued by ALJs of the FCC regarding controversies over FCC regulations. A volume containing a cumulative index is published every three years.

Also increasingly important to attorneys researching administrative law decisions are the online topical databases of WestlawNext and Lexis Advance. Both have numerous databases that contain administrative regulations and decisions.

The final step to researching administrative adjudication is updating. Many agency decisions are included in Shepard's online on Lexis Advance and in KeyCite on Westlaw. These citators cover agency decisions that have been cited in later agency decisions, federal court opinions, state reporters, select law reviews, and several privately published looseleafs.

IV. Summary

Administrative law is primary authority. Missouri administrative rules are compiled both chronologically in the *Missouri Register* and topically in the *Code of State Regulations*, which is accessed through its index. Similarly, federal administrative rules are arranged chronologically in the *Federal Register* and topically in the *Code of Federal Regulations*. Administrative adjudications are less consistently reported, although looseleaf services and online databases are increasingly important sources for locating both agency rules and adjudications.

Chapter 5

Citators

Simply put, a citator is a source that lists all of the authorities that have cited a case, statute, or other legal authority. Once you have located a helpful legal authority, a citator provides you with a list of other sources that have cited to that initial on-point authority.

I. Why Use Citators?

Citators serve two important functions for the legal researcher. First, citators are great *finding tools*. Once you have found an authority that is on point for a legal research problem, citators provide lists of cases, statutes, ALR annotations, law review articles, and other sources that have cited to that initial source. This finding function of citators saves you time and energy by providing lists of good places to look next in your research.

The second important function citators serve is to *update and verify* the continuing validity of the initial source. In case law, for example, a citator's listing provides a history of the case—whether it was affirmed, reversed, reheard, etc.—and an indication of the treatment of the initial case by later cases. By reviewing the history and treatment of a case, you can determine whether it is still good law. While using a citator as a finding tool is an optional research strategy, using a citator to validate the authorities on which you will rely is required.

Both Lexis Advance and WestlawNext provide a citator as part of their online services. Lexis Advance maintains Shepard's and WestlawNext maintains KeyCite. Citators are available for primary authority, including cases, statutes, and administrative regulations, and some secondary sources, such as law reviews.

The following discussion demonstrates how to use citators to update and verify a case and a statute. This process is commonly called "Shepardizing."[1]

---

1. Originally, the only citator was print-based *Shepard's Citations*. Thus, the process

To Shepardize® you must first understand the relevant terminology. In Shepardizing a case, the term "cited case" refers to the case that you want to update
or use to find other authorities. The cited case is the starting point for using
a citator. The "citing authorities" are those later authorities that have referred
to the cited case.

This chapter continues the hypothetical involving a client with a legal problem concerning possession of a bent credit card as a burglar's tool. Assume
you have located the case *State v. Lake*, 686 S.W.2d 19 (Mo. Ct. App. 1984),
which establishes that possession of burglar's tools can be established by possession of tools originally designed for lawful purposes. You want to both verify
and update this case—to make sure it is still "good law"—and find more cases
and other helpful authorities.

II. Shepard's

A. Sheparadizing Cases

Your first step is to sign on to Lexis Advance. After you have logged in and
located an authority, a series of links will be listed on the right of your screen.
Click on the "Shepardize this document" link. You are first sent to the appellate
history of the case. To locate authority that has cited yours, click on either
"Citing Decisions" or "Other Citing Authority" on the left of the screen. Figure
5-1 is the Shepard's result for "Citing Decisions" for the *State v. Lake* case.

After Shepard's processes your citation, your next step is to review the list
of citing authorities. Because later authorities have not frequently cited *Lake*,
its list of citing authorities is not long. You will often, however, encounter
lengthy citing lists. The problem of lengthy citing lists can be alleviated somewhat by certain features of the Shepard's service.

1. Signal Indicators

First, a Shepard's Signal Indicator[2] gives you an at-a-glance indication of
the precedential status of a case. These signal indicators, summarized in Table
5-1, are invaluable in quickly assessing the strength of your case by directing

---

is called "Shepardizing." Shepard's was purchased by Lexis Advance and is now also
available online. If you do not have access to Lexis Advance or to KeyCite on Westlaw,
ask your law librarian to explain how to use print-based Shepard's.

    2. Another way to access Shepard's is to click on the signal indicator found at the top
of the screen when you pull up a case, which will automatically place you in Shepard's.

Figure 5-1. Shepard's® Citing Decisions for State v. Lake

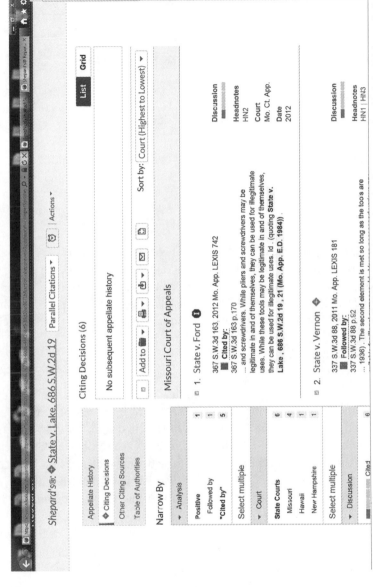

you to specific citing references that may have the most impact on your case. Always remember to check those references yourself. Because a case often contains more than one legal issue, the signal indicator may be referring to an issue that is not implicated in your research. Thus, a case may have a red stop sign but still be good law for your issue.

Table 5-1. Signal Indicators — Shepard's

Red stop sign	Strong negative history or treatment
Yellow yield sign	Significant negative history or treatment
Plus sign within green diamond	Positive history or treatment
Capital "A" within blue circle	Treatment neither positive nor negative
Capital "I" within blue circle	Citing references but no history or treatment

The "Narrow by" link located at the left of the screen allows you to customize your Shepard's report for a more detailed summary of each citing reference displayed. A summary of these references is located in the summary box on the left of your screen. The analyses denoted in bold type in the Shepard's summary box indicate the number of citing references that have cited your case.

2. Analysis Codes

Shepard's editors use these codes to indicate how a cited case has been considered by the citing authorities. Some codes concern the "history" of the cited case, and others concern the "treatment" of the cited case. "History" refers to later opinions regarding the *same case or same parties*, including higher appellate courts that have dealt with the same case. "Treatment" indicates how later cases and other courts have dealt with the *same issues of law* considered in the cited case. To illustrate the distinction between history and treatment, consider "Reversed" and "Overruled." A reversal is part of the subsequent history of the cited case because it indicates that an appellate court reversed or overturned the outcome of the cited case, thus affecting those parties (e.g., the plaintiff, who won below, loses on appeal). "Overruled" indicates that the treatment of the legal issue or point of law by the cited case was overruled by a later court when the issue was raised by a different case and different parties.

Some of the codes provide more critical information than others. For example, it is critical that you know if the case you are updating has been reversed or overruled. It is interesting, but less critical, to know that the case has been discussed in a dissenting opinion. The absence of a code usually indicates that

Table 5-2. Select History and Treatment Codes

History

Affirmed	On appeal, reconsideration, or rehearing, the citing case affirms or adheres to case you are Shepardizing.
Modified	On appeal, reconsideration, or rehearing, the citing case modifies or changes a legal principle in the case you are Shepardizing. This can include affirmance in part and reversal in part.
Reversed	On appeal, reconsideration, or rehearing, the citing case reverses the case you are Shepardizing.

Treatment

Distinguished	The citing case differs from the case you are Shepardizing because it involves dissimilar facts or requires a different application of the law.

the citing case has only referred to the cited case in passing, often as part of a string citation, without discussion or analysis. Table 5-2 lists a sample of these codes.

Remember, editors at Shepard's make these notations. They are helpful indicators of the history and treatment of the cited case but should not be relied upon as authoritative. Shepard's editors are quite literal. If a citing case implicitly, rather than explicitly, overrules the citing case, Shepard's will not place an Overruled before the citing case. Thus, you must read the citing cases yourself to determine the courts' treatment of the cited case. Shepard's only reports; it does not think or analyze for you.

3. Page Number References

As in other citations, the final number in a citation appearing on the citing list refers to a page number. For history cases, the page number reference is to the first page of the citing authority. For treatment cases, the page number reference is the page number on which the cited case appears. This saves you the trouble of digging through the citing authority to find where the case you are checking is cited.

4. Jurisdictions

Another feature that aids the legal researcher in tailoring a Shepard's search is that the jurisdictions are listed separately. Citing authorities start first with cases from the same jurisdiction as the cited case. Then federal courts are listed, separated by level of court and jurisdiction. Then state courts are listed alphabetically.

5. Narrow by Template

Another way to narrow your review is to use the "Narrow by" feature. This feature is an intelligent template that allows you to tailor your results to your needs. The template is "intelligent" in the sense that it provides you with only the history and treatment codes, headnote numbers, and jurisdictions that are represented in the citing references. You can also restrict your results by date.

a. Headnotes

One possible restriction is to use the Narrow by template to restrict citing references to certain headnotes of the original source. The Narrow by template for the *Lake* case lists headnote numbers 1, 2, and 3. The headnote numbers coordinate with the headnote numbers in the published cases. Essentially, the number refers to a specific, numbered headnote in the cited case (in this example, the *Lake* case). When a headnote in a citing reference corresponds to a headnote in the cited case that is particularly relevant to the point of law you are researching, you have found a case that you will definitely want to read. Headnote indicators are an excellent way to narrow your research and pare down long citing lists.

A word of caution, however. Prior to September 1, 2006, Shepard's used headnotes from West's reporter system as well as from the Lexis Advance system. The headnotes are not interchangeable, so researchers had to be sure they were Shepardizing in the set of print Shepard's that corresponded to their version of the cited case. Thus, a point of law might be discussed in headnote 4 in the West version but headnote 9 in the Lexis Advance version. As of September 1, 2006, Shepard's no longer uses West's headnote numbers. The superscript numbers only reference Lexis Advance headnote numbers. If you are doing a citators check on a pre-2006 authority, you will need to be sure that Shepard's is displaying the same version of headnotes that you have in your authority.

Do not be alarmed if there are no additional citing authorities. You will not find a list if no authorities have cited your case.

b. Search Terms

In addition, you can use the "Search Within Results" feature to help you pinpoint issues or facts within the full text of your citing authorities. Search Within Results retrieves a subset of documents from the original Shepard's results that contain the specific terms you enter. You will receive a list of citing references that include the search terms. You can then click on any case name to move directly to the Search Within Results terms in that document.

B. Shepardizing Statutes

Statutes will often be the first primary authority you consult when researching a legal issue, so it is important to learn how to Shepardize them. Shepard's lists of citing authorities for statutes include other statutes, cases, law reviews, Restatements, and ALR annotations that have cited the statute. In this respect, Shepard's works in much the same way as an annotated statutory code, pointing to cases and other authorities that define, amplify, and construe the statute. Shepard's also helps you to verify the continuing validity of the statute by identifying its subsequent history. For example, Shepard's will alert you that the statute was limited by a later statute, repealed, reenacted, revised, or superseded.

Shepard's divides the citing list for each statutory section into its various subsections, subdivisions, and paragraphs. That can be a handy feature if you are specifically interested in only one subsection of the statute. Even if you are interested in Shepardizing a particular subsection of a statute, review the citing list for the statute as a whole first. Citing lists first contain amendments and repeals by act of Congress if any such action has occurred. When no such entries are on a citing list, you can assume that there was no such congressional action during the period covered by this Shepard's volume. Instead of history and treatment codes, the indicators represent legislative action in addition to court decisions, as shown in Table 5-3.

Table 5-3. Select Legislative and Judicial Codes for Shepardizing Statutes

Legislative	
Amended	Statute amended
Repealed	Abrogation of an existing statute
Revised	Statute revised
Judicial	
Constitutional	The citing case upholds the constitutionality of the statute, rule, or regulation you are Shepardizing.
Followed	The citing opinion expressly relies on the statute, rule, or regulation you are Shepardizing as controlling authority.

The same features available when Shepardizing a case using Lexis Advance are also available when Shepardizing a statute. For example, you could use the "Narrow by" list to quickly learn how many times the Eighth Circuit has cited to a certain subsection of a statute. Alternatively, you could use the "Search Within Results" feature to restrict the list of citing references to only cases containing certain terms.

III. KeyCite

Unlike Shepard's, KeyCite originated as an online citator service. Thus, you will find no print sources for KeyCite. KeyCite is only available on Westlaw. Like Shepard's, KeyCite provides both judicial history and subsequent treatment of cited authority.

You can access KeyCite in several ways. Tabs across the top of the authority indicate the various types of citing authority available. The tab is greyed out if no information is available. Another method is to type "KC:" and the citation and you will immediately go to the KeyCite page. In addition, you can click on the status flag that appears on the opening screen of each case. KeyCite's status flags operate similarly to Shepard's signal indicators. A red flag indicates that the case is no longer good law on at least one of its points. A yellow flag indicates some negative history.

A. KeyCite History

KeyCite provides two kinds of history for cases—negative direct history and negative citing references. Negative direct history of the case include all prior and subsequent appellate history. Negative citing references include cases outside of the direct appellate chain that reduce the case's precedential value.

B. Citing References

As in Shepard's, citing references in KeyCite include cases, law review articles, ALR annotations, and treatises. The depth-of-treatment bar indicates how much a citing reference discusses the cited authority. Four squares indicate an extensive discussion, while a single square indicates a mere mention, often in a string citation. KeyCite separates negative citing references from positive references and groups references by depth of treatment. Within each depth-of-treatment group, citing references are ordered by jurisdiction.

You can use the "Narrow" feature to limit the citing references by headnote, jurisdiction, level of court, depth of treatment, date, and document type.

Figure 5-2. KeyCite's Citing References for *State v. Lake*

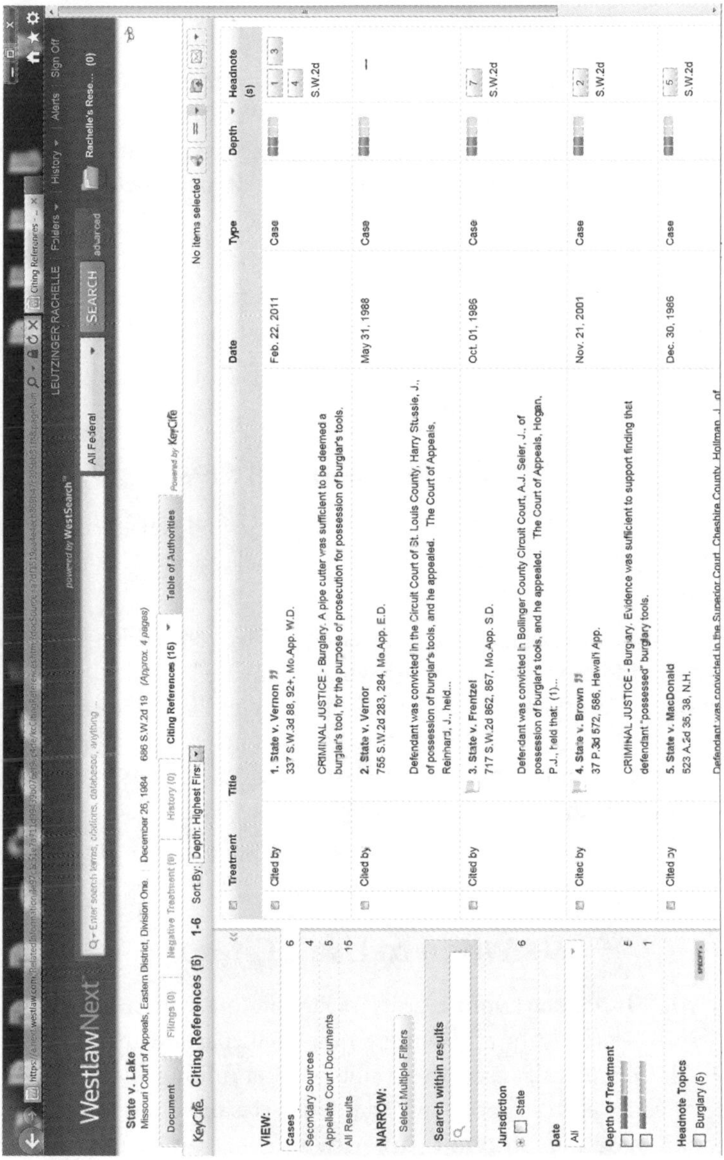

Source: Reprinted with permission of Thomson Reuters.

Another feature of KeyCite is the green quotation marks next to a citing source case. This indicates your cited case was quoted in the citing source. See Figure 5-2 for a screen that illustrates many of these features.

C. KeyCiting Statutes

You can also employ the KeyCite feature when verifying the treatment of a statute. Once you enter the citation in KeyCite, WestlawNext will immediately display the history of the statute. The history flags lists any cases affecting the validity of the statute, recent session laws that have amended or repealed the statute, and proposed legislation.[3]

If you click on the "Citing References" tab next to the "History" tab, WestlawNext will display all of the statute's citing references. You can then restrict your citing list to only specific headnotes, jurisdictions, etc., by using the "Narrow" feature.

IV. Table of Authorities

The Table of Authorities function of Shepard's and KeyCite lists the cases your case has cited. To access this list, simply click on the "TOA" or "Table of Authorities" tab.

Table of Authorities aids your research by telling you hidden weaknesses of your case. A hidden weakness occurs when your case has relied on a case that is no longer good law itself. If that case is not cited by later cases, you may never discover this problem. Table of Authorities helps you by listing the cases your case has used and the status of each of those cases. Thus, you can quickly ascertain whether the law relied on by your case is still good or whether the cases are riddled with yellow or red signals.

V. When to Use a Citator

Since you cannot start your research with citators, you may wonder when during your research is the appropriate time to Shepardize an authority or use KeyCite. This chapter has used these citators after finding an on-point case or a statute to verify each as good law. That illustrates one time to use citators — to verify and update an on-point authority. You may, on the other hand, want to use a citator as a finding tool early in your research to use an authority to find other, possibly more on-point, authorities. You may also want to use citators early in your research because you want to see how much an authority has been considered by other courts and commentators. If, for example, you

---

3. *WestlawNext Help Topics*, www.lawschool.westlaw.com.

are working on a law review article about a certain case or statute, you may use citators to see whether the case or statute has been included in other articles and, if so, how it was treated.

VI. Summary

Citators play a vital role in every research plan. You will use citators as a finding tool and as a source to update and verify the current validity of your research source. Using a citator to verify your authority is required. That is, before you rely on any research, whether in advising a client, drafting a contract, or submitting an appellate brief to a court, checking a citator should always play an integral part in your research.

Citators can expand your research efforts quickly and effectively. Citators can also help narrow your research efforts. The point is not to limit your use of a citator to its traditional function of validating or updating an authority. Remember its additional use as a finding tool.

Chapter 6

Secondary Sources

This chapter examines the use of secondary sources or secondary authority in the legal research process. Secondary sources are not the law; instead, they discuss or analyze primary authorities, including statutes, cases, and rules and regulations, which are the law. Secondary sources are very important in legal research, even though the term *secondary* seems to denigrate their usefulness. In fact, secondary sources will often be your first stop in legal research.

Secondary sources are a good starting point when you know little about an area of law or issue that you are researching. Secondary sources help you acquire a general understanding of the area of law relevant to the research problem. Secondary sources can also help you identify or narrow the relevant legal issues for research. Consulting secondary sources initially yields valuable references or citations to primary authority.

This chapter first discusses five types of general secondary sources: legal encyclopedias, Restatements, treatises and hornbooks, *American Law Reports* (ALR) annotations, and law reviews. These sources discuss all areas of law and all jurisdictions. When beginning a new research project, a researcher may not know the area of law involved. As such, beginning with these general resources is best. In addition to a general understanding of the law, these resources might lead you to Missouri authority.

After discussing these general sources, this chapter focuses on three Missouri-specific secondary sources: Missouri Continuing Legal Education (CLE) Deskbooks, *Missouri Practice Series*, and *Missouri Approved Instructions*. Lastly, this chapter focuses on looseleaf services. Looseleafs are topical compilations of pertinent federal and state statutes, administrative rules and regulations, and relevant court decisions. These services often contain secondary source information as well, including explanations and analyses of issues. Thus, the looseleaf service is a hybrid of primary and secondary source material. As a result, many researchers prefer to use looseleaf services in particular areas of law.

Table 6-1. Outline for Researching Secondary Sources

1. Generate a list of descriptive words.
2. Locate the appropriate secondary source in your library or online.
3. Search the index of the secondary source or run an online search.
4. Read the potentially relevant portion of the secondary source to better understand the issues.
5. Read the surrounding sections for additional relevant explanations.
6. Note the references and citations to primary legal authority.
7. Update the secondary source, if possible.
8. Locate and review the primary authority to which you are referred.

Recognize that there are countless other secondary sources that you will learn about through the secondary sources explained in this chapter, through primary authorities, and through your research experience. The process for researching secondary sources varies depending on the secondary source, but a general outline for performing secondary source research is provided in Table 6-1.

I. Legal Encyclopedias

Legal encyclopedias state basic propositions of law and provide brief explanatory discussions. Encyclopedias typically do not supply detailed legal analysis or explain how various legal rules apply to particular factual settings. Encyclopedias can be used as a research tool in two ways. First, encyclopedias provide background for a particular area of the law, and, second, encyclopedias are a finding tool that leads you to primary authority.

The two most common legal encyclopedias—*Corpus Juris Secundum* (CJS) and *American Jurisprudence 2d* (Am. Jur. 2d)—have national or multi-jurisdictional coverage. Both are multi-volume works arranged alphabetically by subject or topic. Each presents and discusses the majority or prevailing view of legal topics in a narrative form, and each refers to or discusses minority rules or views. Significantly, each encyclopedia supports the narrative with footnotes to primary authorities. Some more populous states have their own legal encyclopedias, including *California Jurisprudence 3d* and *Florida Jurisprudence 2d*. Missouri does not have its own legal encyclopedia. *Missouri Practice Series* covers a range of Missouri-specific topics but is not a comprehensive encyclopedia.

A. *Corpus Juris Secundum*

Corpus Juris Secundum (CJS) is published by West. One advantage of CJS is its cross-referencing to other West publications. For example, CJS provides cross-references to the West key number system by noting the relevant topics and key numbers for the area of law being discussed.[1] CJS's case coverage is more comprehensive than that of its main competitor, Am. Jur. 2d. CJS also provides cross-references to annotations contained in *American Law Reports* (ALR), which is discussed later in this chapter.

1. How to Use CJS

Like other encyclopedias, CJS consists of multiple numbered, bound volumes. The volumes are arranged alphabetically by subject or topic. A "List of Titles in *Corpus Juris Secundum*" is located in the front of each bound volume. Included on this list are the general topics covered in the CJS encyclopedia. A further breakdown is provided by a general outline, followed by a more detailed outline, located at the beginning of each topic section. These outlines provide a systematic organization and classification by section number of the material discussed.

Following the hardbound volumes of CJS is a multi-volume paperbound General Index. In addition, each volume contains its own index in the back. A beginning researcher will typically access CJS by using either the descriptive-word approach or the known-topic approach. If you are unfamiliar with the area of law that a research problem encompasses, you should use the descriptive-word approach and develop a list of words that describe your fact pattern. You will then attempt to locate these words in the General Index volumes of the CJS encyclopedia. The descriptive words that you find in the General Index will refer you to the appropriate topics and sections in CJS.

Using the descriptive-word approach to begin your search for authority on a client's issue involving possession of burglar's tools, you probably could come up with words like "burglary," "tools," and "possession." In the General Index, start with the broadest word, "burglary," and search for other terms as subtopics. Figure 6-1 is an excerpt from the General Index Volume of CJS.

The entry subtopic "Tools" under "Burglary" refers to "Possession of burglar tools or implements, above." That entry refers to several subtopics found in Burglary §§ 49–54. Find the alphabetical, topical volume(s) of CJS that covers

---

1. The topics and section numbers used by CJS do not correspond to the topics and key numbers of West digests; instead, CJS refers you to the specific West topics and key numbers for that topic as a cross-reference.

Figure 6-1. Excerpt from the General Index of CJS

BURGLARY
See also **Larceny** (this index)
Generally, **Burglary § 1-179**

• • •

Burglar tools. Possession of burglar tools or implements, below

• • •

Possession of burglar tools or implements
     generally, **Burglary § 49-54**
     burden of proof, **Burglary § 106**
     character of tools possessed, **Burglary § 53**
     elements of offense, **Burglary § 51-54**
     evidence
          admissibility of evidence, **Burglary § 113, 114**
          weight and sufficiency of evidence, **Burglary § 128-130**
     indictments and informations, above
     instructions to jury, **Burglary § 167**
     intent
          generally, **Burglary § 52**
          evidence, **Burglary § 130**
     issues, proof, and variance, **Burglary § 83**

• • •

Tools. Possession of burglar tools or implements, above

Source: Corpus Juris Secundum, General Index, volume A-B, at 486, 489–90 (2014). Reprinted with permission of Thomson Reuters.

Burglary. You can go directly to these sections, a portion of which is excerpted on the next page as Figure 6-2, or go to the topical outline at the beginning of the Burglary section.

Upon reviewing §§ 49–54, you will learn that possession of burglar's tools includes possessing items adapted for use in a burglary.[2] In CJS, citations to primary authority appear more important than the textual explanation of the basic law. Note the numerous citations to primary authority that are found in CJS in addition to the textual explanation of the basic law.

If, on the other hand, you are reasonably certain that you know the topic or area of law involved in a research problem, you may use the known-topic approach. This approach allows you to refer directly to the relevant topic,

---

2. CJS tells you the same thing about burglar's tools that you learned in Chapter 3 on researching case reporters and digests.

Figure 6-2. Excerpt from CJS Topical Volume

---

§ 53   Kind or character of tools possessed

Under the statutes and case law, any tool may be a burglar tool if it is useful for breaking and entering.

Research References

West's Key Number Digest, Burglary ⬤=12

It is an essential element of the offense of possession of burglar tools that the tools or implements possessed by accused be of the character described in the statute.[1] Generally, under the statutes and case law, any tool may be a burglar tool if it is useful for breaking and entering.[2] Possession of any suitable tools or implements with the requisite intent is sufficient to support a conviction irrespective of whether or not the tools and implements have other and legitimate uses.[3]

[Section 53]

[1]Pa.—Com. v. Stanley, 453 Pa. 467, 309 A.2d 408 (1973).

Tools of housebreaking

N.C.—State v. Vick, 213 N.C. 235, 195 S.E. 779 (1938).

Statutes construed

(1) Under a statute declaring every person having or keeping in his or her possession any tools, implements or other things used by burglars with intent to use them burglariously to be subject to imprisonment, a bottle of nitroglycerin was not among the things the possession of which was made unlawful.

Ky.—Black v. Com., 171 Ky. 280, 188 S.W. 362 (1916).

Source: 12A C.J.S. *Burglary* § 53 (2004). Reprinted with permission of Thomson Reuters.

thereby bypassing the index and, instead, consulting the introductory topic outline to focus your inquiry.

Using the known-topic approach in our example, you would have gone straight to the CJS topical volume(s) covering Burglary and reviewed the topical outline at the beginning of the topic or the individual volume index in the back of that volume to find §§ 49–54.

2. Updating CJS

The topical volumes of the CJS encyclopedia are updated annually with pocket part supplements. These pocket part supplements update the text and footnotes of the entries. When the updating material becomes too voluminous to be neatly contained in the pocket part supplement, a revised volume or volumes of CJS are issued. This revised volume or volumes supersedes and replaces the old volume and its pocket part.

The General Index to CJS is also updated annually by either replacing the paperbound General Index volumes with a new set of paperbound General Index volumes or adding a General Index Update Volume.

B. *American Jurisprudence 2d*

The other general legal encyclopedia is *American Jurisprudence 2d* (Am. Jur. 2d), a green, multi-volume set of books, also published by West. Am. Jur. 2d shares many common features with its counterpart. Like CJS, Am. Jur. 2d divides the whole of American law into several hundred topic areas, which it arranges alphabetically. Am. Jur. 2d also contains a multi-volume paperbound General Index and individual indexes at the end of each volume. Am. Jur. 2d begins each topic section with an explanatory note (including the scope of the topic), a section outline, and cross-references to other publications. Finally, like CJS, each Am. Jur. 2d encyclopedia principally focuses on the prevailing view or majority rule of law.

Some notable differences exist, however, between Am. Jur. 2d and CJS. Am. Jur. 2d takes a more discriminating or selective approach with regard to the case authority it cites as support for its narrative on a given topic. As a result, Am. Jur. 2d contains much more narrative text than CJS, while CJS contains many more cited cases in footnotes. Am. Jur. 2d supplements its references to case authorities with additional cross-references to other publications, including *American Law Reports* (ALR). Also, Am. Jur. 2d provides a more comprehensive treatment of statutory law and the federal rules of procedure. An additional and handy reference to the discussions of statutes is provided by the "Tables of Laws and Rules" contained in each individual volume, as well as in a separate volume of the General Index. This table cross-references federal rules, uniform codes, Restatements, and model codes to the relevant sections of Am. Jur. 2d.

1. How to Use Am. Jur. 2d

The beginning researcher will most likely access Am. Jur. 2d using the descriptive-word or known-topic approach. There will be few, if any, differences in the methodology used to access Am. Jur. 2d and CJS. After you have a list of descriptive words, use the General Index to direct you to a topic that looks promising to resolve the legal issue. Once you have located a promising topic entry, go to the relevant volume and section, and then review the text. Figure 6-3 is an excerpt from the Am. Jur. 2d General Index containing the entry "Burglary."

Figure 6-3. Excerpt from Am. Jur. 2d General Index

BURGLARY
See also **Robbery** (this index)
See also **Theft** (this index)
Generally, **Burglary § 1-72**
• • •
Possession of burglar tools
     generally, **Burglary § 67-72**
     burden of proof, **Burglary § 71**
     constitutional law, **Burglary § 68**
     evidence, **Burglary § 71**
     indictments and informations, **Burglary**
       § 70
     joint and several liability, **Burglary § 69**
     joint possession, **Burglary § 72**
• • •
Tools. Possession of burglar tools, above

Source: American Jurisprudence 2d, General Index, volume B-C, at 197–98 (2014 ed.). Reprinted with permission of Thomson Reuters.

Figure 6-4 on the next page is an excerpt of the Am. Jur. 2d narrative from Burglary section 67. If you felt sufficiently comfortable with the legal issue, you could forego the General Index and individual volume index, and instead use the known-topic approach—simply go to the outline at the beginning of each topic.

2. Updating Am. Jur. 2d

Am. Jur. 2d is updated through the issuance of pocket parts for the updating of the text and footnotes of each topic. The General Index is updated annually by completely replacing the paperback General Index volumes or by adding a separate annual General Index volume.

Figure 6-4. Excerpt from Am. Jur. 2d Topical Volume

---

§ 67   **Generally**

Research References

West's Key Number Digest, Burglary ⊆12
Validity, construction and application of statutes relating to burglars' tools,
   33 A.L.R.3d 798

Burglary and the possession of burglary tools are two distinct and
separate crimes for which two convictions and two sentences are
deemed proper.[1] A person may be convicted and sentenced for both
burglary and the possession of burglary tools when the tool is a common household item, such as a screwdriver, if the evidence shows the
item was used, or was intended to be used, in a burglary.[2] However, a
screwdriver used as a "replacement key" for a vehicle cannot form the
basis for a conviction of possession of burglary tools arising from the
defendant's entry into a vehicle absent evidence that the screwdriver
was used to gain entry into the vehicle.[3]

Source: 13 Am. Jur. 2d *Burglary* § 67 (2009). Reprinted with permission of Thomson Reuters.

3. Other Features of Am. Jur. 2d

A unique feature of Am. Jur. 2d is its "New Topic Service" looseleaf binder.
This feature allows West to respond quickly to significant shifts in doctrine or
newly evolving areas in the law without the wholesale revision and reissue of
existing volumes.

An additional Am. Jur. 2d feature is the "Am. Jur. 2d Desk Book." It serves
as a legal almanac containing a variety of miscellaneous legal information and
facts in the form of charts, graphs, and tables. There are even anatomical draw-
ings that are, presumably, of interest to lawyers in the medical malpractice
area. This Desk Book differs from the Missouri Bar CLE Deskbooks that focus
on one particular subject area.

West has also published what it considers to be related Am. Jur. legal encyclopedias. These related sets are intended to assist in preparing a case for trial
and include *American Jurisprudence Proof of Facts*, *American Jurisprudence
Trials*, *American Jurisprudence Legal Forms 2d*, and *American Jurisprudence
Pleading and Practice Forms, Revised*.

C. Legal Encyclopedias Online

Both CJS and Am. Jur. 2d are available online. On WestlawNext, each encyclopedia has its own database. "Corpus Juris Secundum" includes the current,
updated version of CJS, and "American Jurisprudence 2d" includes the same

information for Am. Jur. 2d. In addition, WestlawNext has databases that combine various secondary sources by topic.

Similarly, on Lexis Advance, "American Jurisprudence 2d" contains Am. Jur. 2d. Lexis Advance also has sources that combine secondary sources by topic. CJS does not appear in any Lexis Advance database.

To use the descriptive-word approach, construct a search query as explained in Chapter 8 to use in your selected database. To use the known-authority approach for legal encyclopedias online, enter the Am. Jur. 2d citation in the search box on either Lexis Advance or on WestlawNext. Enter the CJS citation only on WestlawNext. Use the "Book Browse" feature on Lexis Advance or the "Previous Section" and "Next Section" feature on WestlawNext to review the sections before and after the section you entered.

A researcher can also use the known-topic approach for online legal encyclopedias. Just like the topical outline at the beginning of each topic in both print encyclopedias, the online versions also contain a topical index.

II. Treatises and Hornbooks

A second category of secondary authority includes legal treatises and hornbooks. Generally, treatises are research sources that summarize, explain, and critique an area of law. Treatises are typically authored by well-recognized experts in that area of law. Well-known treatises include *Prosser and Keeton on The Law of Torts*, Farnsworth's *Contracts*, Moore's *Federal Practice*, and Wright and Miller's *Federal Practice and Procedure*. Treatises vary considerably in size, number of volumes, and breadth and depth of coverage. Hornbooks are usually single-volume works that offer a more summarized view of the topic.

A. How to Find the Right Treatise

Treatises often will be found in the area of the law library in which other information related to the same subject matter is located. To find a treatise, search an online catalog using a subject, title, or author approach. After finding a title on point, browse the shelves nearby for additional treatises on the same subject.

Simply asking a librarian to provide you with the treatise(s) on reserve for a particular subject matter area of law will often prove quite fruitful.

B. How to Use Treatises and Hornbooks

Once you have selected an appropriate treatise, a logical next step is to carefully examine the table of contents. The table of contents will provide a roadmap of the manner in which the subject matter has been organized and an outline of the various subject areas covered by the author. Often, simply reviewing the table of contents will lead you to the section(s) of the treatise relevant to your research problem. As an alternative to the table of contents approach, you could access the relevant section(s) of the treatise through its index using the descriptive-word approach.

Another possible point of access to relevant section(s) for many treatises and hornbooks is the table of cases. The table of cases provides an alphabetical listing of all cases cited and discussed in the text. On the occasions when you set out on a research project knowing a seminal case related to your research problem, you may be able to find the appropriate section(s) of the work by consulting the table of cases. If the known case has been cited and discussed by the author, it will be listed in the table of cases noting the section(s) and or page number(s) of the text where it is discussed.

C. Updating Treatises and Hornbooks

Not all treatises are regularly updated; indeed, some have never been updated. The print treatises that are updated use different methods. Many use pocket part supplements. Some are published in looseleaf format. This format allows pages to be replaced as needed. Still other treatises and hornbooks are republished as new editions. These updates do not necessarily occur on a regular or annual basis; therefore, you should take care to note the last date on which the work was updated.

D. Other Features of Treatises and Hornbooks

Some treatises and hornbooks are useful as primary authority finders. That is, they are helpful in directing the researcher to relevant statutory or case authority. Typically, treatises will include various seminal cases and will examine them quite thoroughly. Additional related cases are cited in the footnotes.

The *Hornbook Series* of treatises is a West publication. The more recent editions include, at the end of each section, references from which the researcher can derive the appropriate topic and key number in the West system to find material related to the topic or subtopic examined in the hornbook section.

These recent editions also include formatted search queries that can be used to find related primary authority using an appropriate WestlawNext database.

E. Treatises and Hornbooks Online

Many treatises are available online through both WestlawNext and Lexis Advance. WestlawNext maintains the "Texts & Treatises" database that includes multiple treatises and hornbooks. Each individual treatise is also available in its own database, such as "Federal Practice & Procedure" for the Wright & Miller treatise discussed earlier in this chapter.

Lexis Advance also includes treatises in its sources. They are easiest to locate in the source directory. Click on "by Source" and then on the desired topic. The directory is then narrowed to those sources.

III. Restatements of the Law

A Restatement is a work that attempts to summarize or restate American common law in a particular area, such as torts or contracts.[3] The Restatements generally reflect the common law but are not the law of any particular jurisdiction until a specific Restatement section is adopted by that jurisdiction.

In the 1920s many of the most prominent members of the American legal community were concerned that American case law was becoming too complex and unpredictable. To address this growing concern, the American Law Institute (ALI) was organized in 1923. ALI was made up of lawyers, judges, and legal scholars who undertook to simplify and make more certain American common law doctrine. The Restatements have largely succeeded in clearly articulating the accepted rules of law that are often buried in the legal opinions issued by courts of various jurisdictions; the Restatements also propose ways to reconcile differences between jurisdictions.

---

3. The Restatements span three separate series and cover about a dozen areas of law. The first series of Restatements (produced between 1923 and 1944) covered the following areas of law: agency, conflict of laws, contracts, foreign relations law, judgments, property, restitution, security, torts, and trusts. A second series (produced since 1952) has been issued covering all of the original areas except restitution and security. In addition, the Restatement (Second) series also issued a Restatement of landlord and tenant law. A third series of the Restatements was begun in 1986 and features a navy blue binding. To learn the current status of revised and newly proposed Restatements, consult the most recent Annual Report of the American Law Institute at www.ali.org.

Publication of a Restatement typically begins with the assignment of a preeminent legal scholar as the "Reporter" for the subject matter area to be covered by the particular Restatement. The Reporter prepares a preliminary draft containing all the common law for that area of the law, dividing the law into sections. This draft is circulated to American Law Institute members and advisors and to members of various bar associations. After rounds of critiques and often numerous revisions, the final version is approved by the members of the American Law Institute, and the Restatement is issued.

Commentators disagree as to how much or how little weight or authority the Restatements should be given. Courts sometimes explicitly *adopt* a specific section of a Restatement as part of a state's law.[4] Once a Restatement is adopted by a jurisdiction, it becomes primary legal authority. Alone, however, the Restatement is a secondary authority. Even as a secondary authority, the Restatement can be very persuasive to a court considering which legal path to follow.

A. Organization of Restatements

Each Restatement volume begins with a table of contents revealing the organization of the Restatement. Restatements are separated into divisions (each division covers a broad area of law), chapters (each chapter covers one aspect of that broad area), and enumerated sections (each section covers one specific point of law). A citation to a Restatement includes the area of law, the title of the volume, and the section number of the specific point of law. For example, Restatement (Third) of Property (Wills and Other Donative Transfers) § 2.1:

> *Third series* of the Restatement of Property, covering Wills and Other Donative Transfers
> > *Division I*—Probate Transfers (Wills and Intestacy)
> > > *Chapter Two*—Intestacy
> > > > *Section 2.1*—General Principles and Definitions

A particular Restatement section first presents, in black boldface print, the principle or "black-letter" rule of law to be considered. Any well-established exceptions or counter-rules will typically be expressed immediately following the general rule. Following the boldface section, the Reporter's commentary is presented under the heading "Comment." The Comment further explains

---

4. *E.g., Hylin v. United States*, 715 F.2d 1206, 1212 (7th Cir. 1983) (taking judicial notice that Illinois courts have adopted § 324A(a) of the Restatement (Second) of Torts).

Figure 6-5. Excerpt from a Restatement

---

§ **2.1** General Principles and Definitions

(a) A decedent who dies without a valid will dies intestate. A decedent who dies with a valid will that does not dispose of all of the decedent's net probate estate dies partially intestate.

(b) The decedent's intestate estate, consisting of that part of the decedent's net probate estate that is not disposed of by a valid will, passes at the decedent's death to the decedent's heirs as provided by statute.

Comment:

a. Introduction. A decedent who dies without a valid will dies *intestate*. A decedent who dies with a valid will that does not dispose of all of the decedent's net probate estate dies *partially intestate*. A decedent who dies intestate or partially intestate is sometimes called *the intestate* or *the intestate decedent*.

The decedent's intestate estate consists of that part of the decedent's net probate estate (see § 1.1(b)) that is not disposed of by a valid will. The intestate estate passes at the decedent's death to the decedent's *heirs* as provided by statute.

---

the rule set forth, often dissecting the rule phrase by phrase. Figure 6-5 illustrates these features of the Restatement.

Following each section of the Comment are "Illustrations," consisting of one or more hypothetical applications of the rule presented. These Illustrations may prove helpful in resolving or illuminating legal issues.

Beginning with the publication of the Restatements (Second), the Comments and Illustrations are sometimes followed by Reporter's Notes that supply further background on the particular section.[5] Additionally, the Reporter's Notes will contain citations to court decisions and other authorities that are both supportive and contrary to the stated rule.

---

5. This feature, however, is not absolutely uniform. The first three Restatements (Second) published, covering agency, torts, and trusts, do not include this feature. The notes for these Restatements were printed in separate volumes of Appendices, which also included court citations referring to Restatement sections, tentative drafts, and other cross-references.

B. How to Use Restatements

Restatements can be accessed by all three research approaches. Because each Restatement deals with a discrete area of law (tort, property, contract, etc.), it is easy to determine which Restatement to consult based on that broad area of law. Each Restatement has its own index; thus, once you identify the appropriate Restatement, you may go directly to that Restatement's index and use the descriptive-word approach to access the relevant section(s).

Once you are familiar with the organization and content of the Restatements and are confident that you have accurately identified the topic or topics related to your research, the known-topic approach is often quicker to use: bypassing the index, going directly to the table of contents of the particular Restatement, and selecting the appropriate topics for research.

C. Updating the Restatement's Black-Letter Law

The Restatements are updated and revised when a subsequent series is issued on the same subject matter of law. For example, Restatement (Second) of Torts updated and revised the original first series Restatement of Torts. The Restatement (Third) of Torts replaces the Restatement (Second) of Torts. A subsequent series of a particular Restatement both revises and updates existing sections and also adds additional black-letter law sections. Once you have the current Restatement rule for a particular point of black-letter law, you will want to update it in the sense of making sure that the American Law Institute has not revised, or is not in the process of revising, that principle of law. The Restatement's black-letter principles of law are not updated in the now familiar manner of utilizing pocket part supplements. Instead, the American Law Institute provides information on revisions through its website, www.ali.org.

This website has a "Projects" section. That link sends you to a list of all Restatements and uniform laws currently being revised or drafted. Once there, choose the Restatement you are updating, and click on the title. You are then provided the project's purpose, status, meeting schedule, participants, and other details.

D. Finding Case References

What if you want to locate cases that cite to a particular section of the Restatement? One of the most common research uses of the Restatement is using the black-letter law sections of the Restatement to locate cases in a given jurisdiction. In print, use the Restatement Appendix volumes and the pocket parts. The individual Appendices for the individual Restatements contain references to cases that cite specific sections of the Restatements. Since 1975, these Appendices have been updated annually by pocket part supplements.

To locate cases online, access the Restatement through WestlawNext and Lexis Advance. In addition, Restatements are included in each citator, KeyCite and Shepard's, discussed more fully in Chapter 5.

E. Cross-References

Beginning with the Restatement (Second) series, the Restatements have typically supplied helpful cross-references to the West digest system, via topics and key numbers, and to *American Law Reports*.

IV. *American Law Reports*

American Law Reports (ALR) is a hybrid secondary source now published by West.[6] ALR contains articles called "annotations" on a particular point of law written by attorney-editors. ALR also contains a fully reported case illustrating the particular point of law that is the subject of the annotation. Most researchers do not, however, use ALR to find the illustrative reported cases. Instead, researchers use ALR for the annotations, which contain citations to other relevant cases from all jurisdictions that have dealt with the major issue for which the reported case was selected. An ALR annotation tends to give specific, exhaustive information about a narrow area of law. This information and the case citations are what most researchers find helpful.

ALR differs from the legal encyclopedias discussed earlier in that it covers more narrow points of law, but covers each exhaustively.

A. ALR Organization

1. The Reported Case

Illustrative cases concerning certain legal topics in ALR 3d, 4th, and Federal precede each annotation. Beginning with the publication of ALR 5th and Federal

---

6. At this time, ALR consists of the original ALR through ALR 6th, plus ALR Federal and ALR Federal 2d. In 2010, ALR International was added.

2d, however, the illustrative cases are all at the end of each volume. A boldface notation accompanying each annotation sends you to the illustrative case.

The presentation of the reported case is similar to the reporting of opinions in the West reporters. Preceding the printed opinion are a summary of the case and the headnotes. Be aware that the headnotes conform to the Lexis Advance system and will be useful in cross-referencing only to Lexis Advance digests and Shepard's, not to West digests and KeyCite.

2. Title Page of the Annotation

The title page of the annotation includes the title of the particular annotation and the name of the author(s) who wrote the annotation. The authors are attorney-editors. Additionally, the title page contains a helpful summary of the annotation and the illustrative case.

Following the title page is the introductory summary outline showing the organization of the annotation that follows. Next is a "Research References" section that provides cross-references to relevant sections of other resources, including digests, encyclopedias, and form books. ALR provides suggested WestlawNext databases, search queries, and topics and key numbers.

Following the research references are an alphabetically-arranged subject index and a table that depicts represented jurisdictions. This table presents an alphabetical listing of every federal circuit and state jurisdiction that has cases cited in the annotation and includes a full citation of the case. Statutory citations are included in later series to the extent they are addressed in the court opinions. This table also directs you to the relevant section of the annotation that discusses the cited authority of the listed state.

3. Text of the Annotation

Typically, the first few sections of the text of the annotation will be introductory in nature. The usual format is to lead off with a section outlining the scope of the annotation, followed by a section noting related matters,[7] followed by a general overview of the area of law covered by the annotation. The main body of the text provides the author's treatment of the point of law logically organized by sections in a manner that facilitates the examination of the cases selected and cited by the author.

---

7. The "Related Matters" section will usually reference other ALR annotations that deal with similar or closely related topics. This section may also refer to other relevant sources such as law reviews and treatises.

B. How to Use ALR

As with other secondary source material, a variety of approaches can be used for accessing the desired material. This section will use the descriptive-word approach in the more current ALR indexes and digests.

1. Indexes

To access the annotations, use the ALR Index. The ALR Index is a complete index covering all series.

The ALR Index consists of several bound volumes and is updated quarterly by pocket part supplements. Begin by using the descriptive-word approach; the index will refer you to the appropriate annotation(s) for the subject matter being researched, as illustrated in Figure 6-6.

Figure 6-6. Excerpt from ALR Index

BURGLARY
For related topics, *see* **Breaking and Entering; Larceny or Theft; Receiving and Transporting Stolen Property; Robbery; Theft Insurance**
• • •
BURGLARY—Cont'd
Possession of burglar's tools
    admissibility, in prosecution for burglary, of evidence that defendant, after alleged burglary, was in possession of burglarious tools and implements, **143 ALR 1199**
    validity, construction and application of statutes relating to burglars' tools, **33 ALR3d 798, § 7, 8**
• • •
Tools, validity, construction and application of statutes relating to burglars' tools, **33 ALR3d 798**

Source: ALR Index, volume A-B, at 1188, 1190 (2008). Reprinted with permission of Thomson Reuters.

In the event that only a portion of a particular annotation deals with the subject matter listed in the index, the index will refer you to the exact section(s) of the relevant annotation. Remember to update by checking the index pocket part.

A variant of the known-authority approach may also be used to access ALR annotations. The last volume of the ALR Index contains a "Table of Laws, Rules, and Regulations" that provides references to particular annotations that cite various state and federal statutes, rules, and regulations (but not cases). For example, if you know that your research problem deals with a particular Missouri statute, you can consult this table to be directed to the annotation(s) in which that statute is cited.

2. Digests

Remember, the ALR is also a case reporter. As a result, each series has a digest. The ALR Digest covers the ALR 3d through ALR 6th and both ALR Federal series. The digests are similar to their West counterparts in that they subdivide the law into hundreds of topics. As with West, these topics are arranged alphabetically. By referring to the appropriate topic, you will be referred to the relevant annotation. Additionally, the digest will refer you to relevant sections of Am. Jur. 2d and other publications.

This digest system has a significant shortcoming—it does not contain any index. It is sometimes possible for an experienced researcher to refer directly to the digest at the outset of a research project.[8] If you are familiar with only the broad topic area related to your research problem, you may refer to the topic outline at the beginning of every topic or subject matter section of the digest.[9] Consequently, most researchers find the ALR Index far superior to the ALR Digest as a means of locating annotations.

C. Updating ALR

The ALRs are principally updated in two ways: (1) supplementation of an annotation by annual pocket parts and (2) issuance of supplementary and superseding annotations.

---

8. The digest is of limited utility as an independent finding source unless the researcher is familiar with general subject matter areas and sub-areas of the law or familiar with the subject matter and topic organization of the Lexis Advance system. Once the researcher has found a single relevant ALR annotation, however, it is possible to use the appropriate case headnotes to refer to the digest for other relevant annotations.

9. Each topic or subject matter area of the digest is preceded by a brief explanation of its scope and a section-by-section outline of subtopics covered.

Figure 6-7. Annotation History Table

```
┌─────────────────────────────────────┐
│            31 ALR3d 565              │
│    § 16[a], 16[b], Superseded        │
│           38 ALR 6th 97              │
│    § 24, Superseded 51 ALR 6th 219   │
│                                     │
│            34 ALR3d 16              │
│   § 15[a-c], Superseded 53 ALR 6th  │
│                 81                  │
│   ***§ 16[a], 16[b], Superseded     │
│          55 ALR 6th 391             │
└─────────────────────────────────────┘
```

Source: *ALR Index*, volume A-B, at Tables-2 (Supp. Jan. 2015). Reprinted with permission of Thomson Reuters.

Sometimes developments in an area of law are so substantial that updating through the use of a pocket part is inadequate or impractical. In such cases, ALR will issue a *supplementary* or *superseding* annotation. A *supplementary* annotation will typically be issued to discuss a new development in an area of law that was not considered in the original annotation. Larger scale changes or developments to areas of law originally discussed in the annotation are revised with the issuance of a *superseding* annotation.

The occurrence of such supplementary or superseding annotations will be noted in the annual pocket part supplements. Additionally, the information is available in the "Annotation History Table." The Annotation History Table can be found in the last volume of the ALR Index. It provides a numerical listing, by annotation and series, of all annotations that have been supplemented or superseded. The Annotation History Table is kept current in the pocket part supplement that updates the last volume of the ALR Index. Figure 6-7 is an excerpt from an Annotation History Table.

D. ALR Online

Both Lexis Advance and WestlawNext provide online access to ALR. Each service maintains ALR as its own database entitled "American Law Reports." WestlawNext also subdivides this database into topic specific databases such as "American Law Reports-Family Law" and "American Law Reports-Real Property."

V. Legal Periodicals

A. Types of Periodicals

Legal periodicals include law reviews, law journals, and bar journals.[10] Law reviews and law journals (the terms are interchangeable) are scholarly journals published on a periodic basis, often by law school faculty or students. Typically, law reviews publish articles written by legal academicians and practitioners, as well as by law students. Student works are often called "notes" or "comments." In addition, law reviews may contain tributes, essays, and book reviews. Some law reviews are general, publishing articles concerning a wide variety of legal topics, while others focus their content on a more specific area of the law such as environmental law or business law. Table 6-2 on the next page lists law reviews and journals published by law schools in Missouri.

Law review articles, particularly those published in journals with solid reputations in a legal community, are highly revered by academicians, practitioners, and even the courts. They may contain insightful examinations of "cutting edge" and newly developing legal issues. Articles often provide the most thorough and critical analysis of legal issues, significant cases, and legislation. In addition, law review articles provide a fertile repository of related primary and secondary authority. The advantage of locating a recent law review article on an issue you are researching is that someone has already gathered, in one place, much of the relevant legal authority related to your problem.

While law review articles, like other secondary sources, collect and report in one place the results of previous research on a topic, a significant limitation is that law review articles are independent works selected for publication and edited (often by law students) on an ad hoc basis and, as such, are not systematically updated or revised. If you find an article directly on point and stop your search, you may not learn that the law has drastically changed since the law review article was written.

Another limitation of law review articles is that they are not fungible. They vary greatly in philosophical approach, scope, and quality. While a few law journals use a peer review process akin to that of scientific journals, most law reviews are student-run and student-edited. As a result, some articles may be

---

10. Legal periodicals include bar association publications, legal newspapers, and legal newsletters. Non-legal periodicals may also be relevant to a particular project. These include other scholarly journals, commercial newsletters, magazines, and regular newspapers.

Table 6-2. Law Reviews and Law Journals Published by Missouri Law Schools

Journal of the American Academy of Matrimonial Lawyers	University of Missouri-Kansas City
Journal of Dispute Resolution	University of Missouri-Columbia
Journal of Health Law & Policy	Saint Louis University
Missouri Environmental Law & Policy Review	University of Missouri-Columbia
Missouri Law Review	University of Missouri-Columbia
Public Law Review	Saint Louis University
Saint Louis University Law Journal	Saint Louis University
UMKC Law Review	University of Missouri-Kansas City
The Urban Lawyer	University of Missouri-Kansas City
Warsaw Transatlantic Law Journal	Saint Louis University
Washington University Global Studies Review	Washington University
Washington University Journal of Law and Policy	Washington University
Washington University Law Review	Washington University

well-researched and reasoned, comprehensive, and objective, while others may be little more than cursory advocacy of a certain point of view. Therefore, like other secondary sources, law review articles are typically more valuable as a beginning, rather than an end, to the research process.

Another type of legal periodical is the bar journal. Many state and local bars, including Missouri, publish a bar journal that is automatically sent to members of that state's bar. Bar journals are often magazine-like and include bar news, columns by bar officers or members, legal notices, and articles on issues of interest to practicing lawyers. Because the articles appearing in a bar journal are directed to practicing lawyers, as opposed to academicians, they are often shorter and less heavily footnoted than articles in law reviews.

The *Journal of The Missouri Bar* is published bi-monthly. An index is published annually as part of the November–December issue. In addition to a subject matter index, this issue includes a separate author index and case index. Unlike some states' bar journals, the *Journal of The Missouri Bar* covers a wide range of topics, and the articles are significantly footnoted.

B. How to Locate and Use Legal Periodicals

Most of the legal journals referred to as law reviews or law journals are accessible in a variety of ways. This section will deal with the *Index to Legal Periodicals and Books*, *Legal Resources Index* (LegalTrac) and a hybrid finding and locating tool, HeinOnline.[11]

1. Indexes

Law review articles are indexed according to an alphabetical listing by subject and by author's last name. These indexes also contain tables of cases and statutes treated in law review articles.

a. Index to Legal Periodicals and Books

The *Index to Legal Periodicals and Books* (formerly, and more familiarly, called the *Index to Legal Periodicals*) catalogs approximately 500 legal periodicals published from 1926 to the present. This print index combines listings by subject and author and arranges them alphabetically. You will most often conduct a search in this index by using the known-topic approach. Once you have identified the appropriate topic, the index will refer you to the law

---

11. Obviously, there are other methods for finding law review articles. As noted in other chapters, law review articles may be mentioned in certain digests or in other secondary sources. Articles can be found using a citator. Additionally, other indexing schemes may be consulted: *Criminal Justice Periodical Index*, *Current Index to Legal Periodicals*, *Index to Federal Tax Articles*, *Index to U.S. Government Periodicals*, *Index to Foreign Legal Periodicals*, and *Index to Periodical Articles Related to Law*. Other online sources exist, such as Google Scholar and the Social Science Research Network (SSRN).

review, by the journal's volume and page number, where the desired article can be found.

In addition to the combined subject and author section of the index, each volume of the *Index to Legal Periodicals* also contains a Table of Cases Commented Upon. This section provides an alphabetical listing of cases upon which articles in law reviews and other legal periodicals have been written. A similar section is provided as a Table of Statutes Commented Upon. This section is divided into federal, state, and foreign parts, each of which alphabetically lists entries by the name of the relevant act. A separate index section is also provided for book reviews. The *Index to Legal Periodicals* is made up of cumulative one-year and three-year volumes, which are supplemented by monthly pamphlets.

b. LegalTrac

LegalTrac indexes articles published in over 800 legal periodicals from 1980 to the present. LegalTrac is available on computer terminals in many law libraries. The advantage of using LegalTrac is that it merges into a single alphabetical listing the subject index, author/title index, Table of Cases Commented Upon, and Table of Statutes Commented Upon. The listing is accessed when you formulate and enter descriptive-word queries. LegalTrac is updated monthly, obviating the need to check cumulative annual supplements or the monthly paper pamphlet supplements.

2. Finding the Appropriate Journal

Once you identify a particular article and the journal in which it appears, the next step is to determine whether the desired journal is among your law library's hard copy holdings. Most law libraries publish a list of law journals available in print. The listings refer you to the journal's call number, which indicates where in the library the journal will be found. Alternatively, use one of the online databases of Lexis Advance, WestlawNext, or HeinOnline.

At this time, neither WestlawNext nor Lexis Advance has full coverage of all law review articles dating before 1994.[12] After 1994, significant numbers of law reviews are available. You can search some Missouri law reviews individually on WestlawNext. For example, "Missouri Law Review" and "University of Missouri-Kansas City Law Review" are separate databases that contain only

---

12. If the journal you seek is not held by your law library and is before 1994, in most cases, with a librarian's assistance, the desired journal (or at least a copy of the desired article) can be attained through a loan from another library.

that specific law review. Lexis Advance also has separate sources for each journal of Saint Louis University School of Law.

3. HeinOnline

HeinOnline is a paid-subscription, hybrid service for locating and accessing legal periodicals. It provides full-text searching in addition to author/title searching of a great number of law journals. Its website, home.heinonline.org, lists the journals included and periods of coverage. While HeinOnline originally provided historical researchers access to older law journals, the service has now expanded to cover hundreds of journals, with the coverage varying according to the journal. Many academic law libraries subscribe to HeinOnline in lieu of hard copy subscriptions to individual law journals and make its database of legal periodicals available to researchers.

VI. Secondary Sources Specific to Missouri

Like other states, Missouri has several secondary sources specific to Missouri law available to legal researchers. Some of these sources are the product of the organized bar in the form of multi-volume treatises authored by bar members and sold by The Missouri Bar. Other secondary sources include published Continuing Legal Education (CLE) materials.

A. The Missouri Bar CLE Deskbooks

One of the most useful starting points when researching an issue of Missouri law is a series of books published by The Missouri Bar called Missouri CLE Deskbooks. This resource consists of nearly fifty different titles (some titles consist of several volumes) organized by broad subject matter, such as real estate practice, family law, or criminal practice, and then comprised of multiple chapters of a more specific nature, such as easements or mechanics liens. Each chapter is written by a Missouri practicing lawyer, judge, or law professor who is knowledgeable in that area of law. Although the content and organization of a given chapter may vary depending on the author of that chapter, most of the chapters set out, in highly readable narrative form, the Missouri law in the relevant area.

Although the Deskbooks are not exhaustive case or statute finders, the reader is usually pointed to relevant primary authority to illustrate the law discussed. The known-authority approach can then be used to locate additional cases or statutes on point. Of considerable value are the forms that are included in many of the titles in the Deskbook series. Several of the Deskbooks are also available online on Lexis Advance and Loislaw, another subscription service. The Deskbooks are included in The Missouri Bar's free online research service, Fastcase.

The Deskbooks (or a given chapter) are not updated on a regular schedule, nor is there a schedule of pocket part supplementation. Chapters and volumes are updated sporadically by means of supplements. New titles and chapters are added when a need is perceived.

B. *Missouri Practice Series*

Another extremely valuable secondary source for Missouri law is the multiple volume *Missouri Practice Series* (the "Series") authored by Missouri lawyers, judges, and law professors and published by West. The Series serves as a practical guide for Missouri lawyers by thoroughly covering a range of Missouri-specific topics.

The Series includes titles addressing substantive practice areas such as Missouri evidence, criminal law, family law, and probate. In addition to annotated text that explains the Missouri law on a topic, the Series provides illustrative case citations and even legal forms. Some titles are organized by subtopic and others by sections of RSMo. For example, *Missouri Probate Law and Practice* is organized by sections of the Missouri Probate Code. It explains the code section and provides case analysis and citations to relevant cases. Relevant sections of the Series may be accessed by using the descriptive-word approach in the Series' General Index. In addition, each title of the Series contains its own index and the Series is available online on WestlawNext.

C. *Missouri Approved Instructions*

To learn the elements of a crime or cause of action in Missouri, use jury instructions. This resource will help you to more efficiently gauge the strength of a case and to prepare the evidence to prove it.

The Missouri Supreme Court enacts and modifies required jury instructions, called *Missouri Approved Instructions* (MAI), for both civil and criminal cases. After enactment by an order of the Missouri Supreme Court, MAI are published, in reverse chronological order, on the Court's website at www.courts.mo.gov along with the Committee Comment and a Note on Use. There is no index to MAI on the Court's website, and locating an instruction requires opening each order to check its contents. While the Court does not prepare or publish any compilation of MAI for civil cases, it does compile its criminal instructions, and they are available from the Court for a fee. Compilations of MAI for civil cases are available commercially, including West's *MAI, Civil*. This compilation is easier to use to access relevant jury instructions because it contains both a Summary of Contents, which is a table of contents located at the beginning of the volume, and an index. This compilation is available online on WestlawNext.

VII. Looseleaf Services

Looseleaf services are available in virtually all specialized areas of law, including tax, bankruptcy, trade regulations, federal securities, oil and gas, aviation, and labor law. This list names only a few. Many more can be found arranged by subject matter throughout the library, usually shelved with treatises. For a listing of looseleafs available, use the reference book *Legal Looseleafs in Print*.[13] The most prevalent publishers of looseleaf materials are Commerce Clearing House (CCH), the Research Institute of America (RIA), and the Bureau of National Affairs (BNA).

Looseleaf information in publications from these companies is provided much faster than in comparable government publications. Because these subject matter services are in looseleaf binders or notebooks (hence their name "looseleafs"), updating is done on a page-by-page basis. The looseleaf format allows the publisher to send updates frequently and quickly; the outdated pages are removed as new pages are inserted on a regular basis. In addition to replacing outdated pages, publishers will insert additional information on new pages— even in the middle of the volume. As a result, instead of indexes referring a researcher to a page number, looseleaf services typically refer to paragraph or section numbers.

The organizational scheme varies from looseleaf to looseleaf. Some are organized by subject and some by date. The *American Law of Product Liability* is arranged in part by product; entries range from hair spray to car batteries. A looseleaf service may fill one volume or several.

Many looseleafs are available online as subscription services, on WestlawNext, and on Lexis Advance. Some of these electronic looseleafs follow the organization of their print counterparts, while others are similar to other online databases.

---

13. Arlene L. Eis, *Legal Looseleafs in Print 2008* (2008).

As with other research, where to start depends upon what you already know about the issue. The known-topic approach is most effective when researching looseleafs, but you must know which service to use for a particular topic. For example, assume your client needs information regarding filing a state claim for sex discrimination based on her employer's unfair employment practices. You could go to U.S.C. to research federal statutes, *Federal Practice Digest 4th* to research federal cases, CFR to research federal administrative regulations, RSMo to research Missouri statutes, *Missouri Digest 2d* to research state cases, and CSR to research Missouri administrative regulations. Or, you could use the *BNA Labor Relations Reporter* looseleaf service to locate everything in one source — one-stop shopping.

Attorneys practicing in specialized areas of the law often utilize looseleaf services as their primary research tool. Looseleaf services provide almost everything needed to research an area of law. Looseleafs are updated frequently, making them highly efficient resources for attorneys practicing in specialized areas of law.

VIII. Summary

Secondary sources are invaluable research tools with a variety of research techniques. Secondary sources are of great value in the beginning stages of a research project and should be used at that point. Remember, however, that while these sources often provide a rich and fruitful beginning to your legal research, particularly when researching an area with which you are unfamiliar, they rarely are the stopping point. Do not forget that these sources, unless expressly incorporated into the law of a jurisdiction, are neither primary nor binding authority. They are not the law. At best, the court will look upon them as persuasive.

Chapter 7

Legislative History and Legislation

I. What Is Legislative History, and When Do You Use It?

This chapter introduces an area of mixed primary and secondary authority known as legislative history. The term "legislative history" refers to all the documents created during the process of drafting, debating, and finally enacting a statute. Legislative history can be a primary source of law because it includes some documents that represent the law itself, such as the final statute passed by the legislative body and signed by the executive. For the most part, however, legislative history consists of secondary authority: reports and documents that explain or trace the history of a statute as it worked its way through the legislative process.

Legislative history exists for federal statutes and for the statutes of some states. The federal government publishes and makes available fairly complete documents that trace the process by which a bill becomes a law. Many pages of documents are created in this legislative process. Many of these documents are published by the government and are accessible to the legal researcher who wants to learn more about a particular bill or law. Many states, however, including Missouri, have no accessible trail of legislative history to research. The documents produced are not readily available. What a researcher can do to research Missouri legislative history is to locate copies of Missouri legislative bills and track pending bills that are still in the legislative process.

When a legislature drafts and passes a statute, it presumably tries to carefully choose words that denote the intended purpose of the law. Occasionally, however, the language used by the legislature in a statute is not clear or is ambiguous in some way. Or, when a statute has been amended multiple times over the years, the resulting language can become a patchwork that produces ambiguity when viewed as a whole. This ambiguity creates uncertainty and leads to lawsuits between parties who disagree on what the statute means. When this uncertainty arises, courts attempt to resolve it, first, by gleaning the purpose or intent of the legislature in passing the statute and then by following or carrying out that intent.

For example, suppose a state statute reads, "No motor vehicles are allowed in state parks."[1] Under this statute, would an ambulance driver violate the statute by going into the park to aid a patron? Would a person using a motorized wheelchair be allowed access to the park? One person might define "motor vehicle" as any vehicle intended for transport and powered by an engine, while another person might believe that the term does not apply to emergency vehicles or wheelchairs. When an ambiguity or uncertainty exists in the wording of a statute, the court looks to the intent of the legislature. What did the legislature want to happen when it enacted this statute? Did it want to keep parks quiet and clean? The court may consider the legislature's original intent when interpreting an ambiguity.

Legislative history is an important source of information concerning the legislature's intent. By researching the text of the original bill, proposed amendments, committee and subcommittee reports, and floor debates, a researcher can often determine what the legislature wanted to accomplish and why it chose the specific language used. In addition, witness statements in legislative hearings allow researchers to see what information the legislature had available to it when it enacted a statute.

Researching legislation and legislative history are quite similar. The researcher is seeking the documents at each stage of the legislative process. The difference is that legislation research is searching for documents prior to the bill's enactment while legislative history is looking for the same documents after the bill's enactment. Thus, a researcher must first understand the legislative process and the documents that form a traceable legislative history whether prior to or after a bill's enactment.

II. Missouri Legislation

Missouri's constitution vests the power to legislate to "The General Assembly of the State of Missouri."[2] The General Assembly is composed of the Senate and the House of Representatives.

---

1. This is a much-cited, traditional statutory analysis example attributed to H.L.A. Hart.

2. Mo. Const. art. III, § 1.

A. Introduction of a Bill

The legislative process for the Missouri General Assembly begins with a proposed law, referred to as a bill. Bills may originate in either the Senate or the House of Representatives. Except for general appropriations bills,[3] bills cannot contain more than one subject, cannot be amended in their passage through either house in a way that changes their original purpose, and cannot be introduced in either house after the sixtieth legislative day of a session without the consent of a majority of the elected members of each house.

A bill may be introduced by any senator or representative during the legislative session. The bill may be written by the legislator or drafted by the staff of the Committee on Legislative Research at the request of a senator or representative. When introduced, a bill is assigned a number and read by title for the first time by the Senate or House reading clerk. After placement on the calendar for second reading, the President Pro Tem of the Senate or the Speaker of the House (depending upon the originating house) assigns the bill to a committee. The committee may then hold a public hearing.

The committee may (1) report the bill with the recommendation "Do Pass"; (2) recommend passage with committee amendments, which are attached to the bill; (3) return the bill without recommendation; (4) substitute a new bill known as a "committee substitute in lieu of the original bill"; (5) report the bill with a recommendation "Do Not Pass"; or (6) make no report at all.

B. Perfection of a Bill

When a bill is reported favorably out of committee or a substitute is recommended, the bill is placed on the "perfection calendar" and debated on the floor of the originating house. If a substitute bill is recommended by the committee or if committee amendments are attached to the bill, the substitute or the amendments are first presented, debated, and voted upon. Further amendments can then be proposed by other members. These changes are designated as House or Senate amendments to differentiate them from the committee amendments. A motion is made to declare the bill perfected after all amendments have been considered. If passed by a majority of the originating house, the bill is then reprinted.

---

3. Appropriations bills determine how state revenues are spent.

C. Final Passage of a Bill

After perfection and reprinting, the bill goes on the calendar for a third reading and final passage. When the bill is reached in the order of the legislative body's daily business, any member may speak for or against its passage. However, no further amendments of a substantive nature can be offered. A constitutional majority of the elected members (eighteen in the Senate and eighty-two in the House) is required for final passage.

Upon passage, the bill is then reported to the other house. It is read a second time, referred to a committee of that house for hearing, reported by committee, and offered for final approval. If further amendments are approved, they are reported to the originating house with a request that the changes be approved. A conference may be requested if the originating house does not approve of the changes. Members from each house are designated to serve as a joint conference committee and to discuss the changes. Upon agreement by the joint conference committee, the originating house acts first on the joint conference committee version of the bill. If approved, it goes to the other house. If approved there, the bill is declared "Truly Agreed to and Finally Passed." If either house rejects the conference committee bill, it may be returned to the same joint conference committee or a new joint committee may be appointed for further conferences. Upon final passage, a bill is ordered enrolled, typed in its finally approved form, and printed.

D. Signing of a Bill

Bills Truly Agreed to and Finally Passed are then signed in open session by the House speaker and Senate President or President Pro Tem. At the signing, any House or Senate member may file written objections, which are sent with the bill to the Governor.

E. Governor's Actions

The Governor has fifteen days to act on a bill sent to him during the legislative session. If the legislature has adjourned or has recessed for a thirty-day period, he has forty-five days to act on the bill. If the Governor signs the bill, it becomes law. If the Governor vetoes the bill, it is returned to the originating house with his objections. The General Assembly can override the Governor's veto with a two-thirds vote by members of both houses. If any bill is not acted on by the Governor within these time limits, the bill becomes law in the same manner as if the Governor had signed it.

F. Effective Date of a Law

The Missouri Constitution provides that no law passed by the General Assembly can take effect until ninety days after the end of the session in which it was enacted, except in case of an emergency. Some bills specify the exact date they take effect.

G. Duties of the Secretary of State

The Secretary of State preserves the final typed copy of the signed bill, now called a *law*. All the laws created in a session are bound together at the close of that session into one volume, entitled *Laws of Missouri*. The Revisor of Statutes in the Office of the Committee on Legislative Research then codifies the laws into the general statutes. This code is referred to as *Revised Statutes of Missouri*.

III. Compiling Missouri Legislative History

A. Committee Reports

No single resource provides the legislative history for Missouri statutes. Moreover, the General Assembly does not publish any committee hearings or reports for public access. All materials of this sort must be requested directly from the committee chair for the session in which the bill was considered.

Contact information for committees of the current legislative session is available on the Senate's website, www.senate.mo.gov, and the House of Representative's website, www.house.mo.gov. Both of these websites have links to the committee directories and each committee's assigned bills.

Past session hearings or reports vary in their availability and can be difficult or impossible to access. Success will depend on whether the individual chairperson or sponsor of the bill personally maintained a copy. For information on past committees, use the *Official Manual of the State of Missouri*, commonly referred to as the "Missouri Blue Book," to access committee directories. If the individual is still a member of the General Assembly, the current contact information can be obtained from the directories found on the Senate's or House of Representative's websites or by using the current Missouri Blue Book.

B. Prior Print Versions of the Bill

In Missouri, researching the different versions of a bill as it progressed through the legislative process to enactment is much easier than locating com-

Table 7-1. Reverse Chronological Order of Missouri Legislative Bills

- Statutory Code
- Final Typed Copy (session law)
- As Signed Bill
- Truly Agreed to and Finally Passed Bill
- Committee Perfected Bill
- As Introduced Bill

mittee reports. The changes between the As Introduced bill and the Truly Agreed to and Finally Passed bill reflect changes made after the committee's consideration and then after each house's debates. Any changes made by the conference committee before final passage might also lead to arguments about the current language's interpretation.

Compile the legislative history of your bill by working in reverse chronological order of your bill's progression through the legislative process as shown in Table 7-1. Essentially, you are piecing together the bill's changes to determine if the changes, either deletions or additions, impact your interpretation of the current law's language.

Begin with either *Revised Statutes of Missouri* or *Vernon's Annotated Missouri Code*. Immediately following the statutory text, both publishers provide key legislative history information. At a minimum, they provide the bill number and legislative year of enactment. They may also provide the exact page number of the bill where the statutory language is provided and the effective date of the statute. Figure 7-1 illustrates Missouri's possession of burglar's tools statute; the legislative history is provided immediately after the statute's language and is enclosed in parentheses. This statute began as Senate Bill No. 60 in the 1977 legislative session and can be found on page 662 of *Laws of Missouri*. Note the Historical and Statutory Notes that reference prior laws and revisions.

With the bill number, you can proceed directly to *Laws of Missouri* for the year the bill was enacted. *Laws of Missouri* is a chronological compilation of the bills passed in each legislative session. This source will give you the language of the session law. If you do not have the bill number, *Laws of Missouri* has tables and indexes to help you find the bill number when you know the year of enactment and the popular name of the act, the statutory section number, or the subject.

Figure 7-1. *Vernon's Annotated Missouri Code* § 569.180 RSMo 1999

569.180.   Possession of burglar's tools

1. A person commits the crime of possession of burglar's tools if he possesses any tool, instrument or other article adapted, designed or commonly used for committing or facilitating offenses involving forcible entry into premises, with a purpose to use or knowledge that some person has the purpose of using the same in making an unlawful forcible entry into a building or inhabitable structure or a room thereof.

2. Possession of burglar's tools is a class D felony.

(L.1977, S.B. No. 60, p. 662, § 1, eff. Jan. 1, 1979.)

Comment to 1973 Proposed Code

The section replaces § 560.115 RSMo and is based on New York Penal Code § 140.35. The section makes clear that purpose to use the tools for an unlawful entry of knowledge that someone else will so use them is required for guilt. This should require considerably more than simply evidence of prior arrests or reputation.

Historical and Statutory Notes

Prior Laws and Revisions:	
Mo.R.S.A. § 560.115.	R.S.1919, § 3306.
R.S.1939, § 4449.	R.S.1909, § 4529.
R.S.1929, § 4057.	R.S.1899, § 1892.

Source: *Vernon's Annotated Missouri Statutes*, volume 41, page 387 (2000). Reprinted with permission of Thomson Reuters.

Prior print versions of the bill are available in government depository libraries, such as the Missouri Supreme Court Library, the University of Missouri Law Library, and the Leon E. Bloch Law Library of the University of Missouri-Kansas City School of Law. The heading of the bill will note the bill's stage in this process (e.g., introduced, perfected) and will state all actions upon it up to that point in time. Some libraries will bind together the bills received for one session, but no indexing system is available. Thus, a researcher must rely on the bill number and year of enactment to locate prior versions of bills in print.

C. Journals

Other available resources in a government depository library are the *House Journal* and *Senate Journal*. These journals are published each day the General Assembly is in session. They provide the calendars of bills, notations of motions and actions, and roll call votes but do not provide a record of debates or committee hearings.

D. *Vernon's Missouri Legislative Service*

To research more current legislation, start in *Vernon's Missouri Legislative Service*. This is a chronological compilation of the newest laws prior to their incorporation in *Revised Statutes of Missouri*. *Vernon's Missouri Legislative Service* is published several times each year in pamphlet form by West. West assigns its own number to each law to allow a chronological sequencing in the pamphlets. Note that West's number does not match the bill number assigned when the bill was introduced in the General Assembly. Also note that these pamphlets are not cumulative, though their indexing features are.

When starting with the statute number, look first at the "Statutes Amended, Repealed, etc. Table" in the most recent pamphlet to see if any changes have been made to your statute. This table will give you the West number, the bill number, the originating house, and the effect of the recent bill on the statute (e.g., amended, repealed). When you already know the bill number, use the "Table of House and Senate Bills Approved and Joint Resolutions," which is tabulated by the bill number and provides the West number. Other features in *Vernon's Missouri Legislative Service* include a "Table of Court Rules" and a subject index. Thus, if you did not know either the statute number or the bill number, you could use research terms in the subject index to locate recent legislation.

Using the West number, you can locate the legislation in the proper pamphlet of *Vernon's Missouri Legislative Service*. One advantage of this legislative service is that the printed bill is redlined, meaning deletions and additions are indicated by strikeouts and underlining. The redlining shows exactly what language was changed in the legislative process.

E. Online Access to Bills

Without question, online bill research is more efficient than searching for various prior print versions of bills. One drawback to online research is that access is limited to bills passed within the last ten to fifteen years.

1. Free-Access Sources

The website of the General Assembly at www.moga.mo.gov provides information for statutes enacted since 1995 through the link "Joint Bill Tracking." This information is searchable by keyword through a "Basic Search" or an "Advanced Search." The Basic Search scans House and Senate bill cover sheets. The *cover sheets* include information on the House or Senate bill number, bill titles, sponsor, and co-sponsors. The Basic Search also includes a general subject matter search. The Advanced Search scans all data for a specific year including cover sheets plus all House and Senate bill text, bill summaries, amendments, fiscal notes, committee reports, courtesy resolutions, and member data pages.

2. Fee-Based Sources

Commercial online services also provide bill tracking data. WestlawNext maintains the "Missouri Legislative History" database that provides information on acts and joint resolutions; "Missouri Bill Tracking" includes summaries and the status of bills; "Missouri Journals" includes the House and Senate journals since 1999; and "Missouri Governor's Messages" includes the Governor's messages and press releases since 2001.

Lexis Advance has similar databases, accessible through its directory. "Missouri Advance Legislative Service" includes the full text of all laws passed during the most recent legislative session; "Missouri Full-Text Bills" includes pending legislation; "Missouri Bill Tracking Reports" consists of summaries of pending legislation; and "Missouri Bill Tracking and Full-Text Bills" is a combination of the summaries and full-text of bills of the current session. "Missouri Legislative Bill History" includes bill analyses and committee reports, if available.

F. Summary

Researching Missouri legislative history is unfortunately limited to prior versions of bills. The most critical aspect of legislative history—changes in the actual language of the bill—is available from *Vernon's Missouri Legislative Service*, *Laws of Missouri*, government depository libraries' collections of prior versions of bills, and online resources.

IV. Federal Legislation

The federal legislative process parallels Missouri's legislative process.

A. Referred Print

The first step in the legislative process is the introduction of a bill by a legislator into one of the two chambers of Congress: the House or the Senate. In most cases, a bill may originate in either chamber, though appropriation bills must originate in the House of Representatives. When a bill is introduced, it is assigned a letter and a number for organizational purposes. Bills introduced in the House of Representatives carry "H.R." and a number (e.g., H.R. 5463).

Senate bills have "S." as a prefix (e.g., S. 7896). This number remains with the bill until the bill is passed or until the end of the congressional session. The bill number is used to track the bill as it moves through the legislative process.

This first version of the bill is called the *referred print* of the bill. The referred print is helpful because it can be compared with later versions of the bill, including the bill finally enacted, to show the intent of Congress. In theory, any changes between the referred print and the final text of the statute were made by the legislature to accomplish a specific purpose.

B. Committee Hearings

Once a bill is introduced, it is referred to a committee within the originating chamber (e.g., the Armed Services Committee) for consideration and debate. The committee may in turn refer the bill to a subcommittee. The committee's job is to analyze and consider the bill in terms of its impact on federal agencies and the public and then to make a recommendation to the full chamber on whether to enact the bill into law. Most of the consideration of a bill occurs in committee and most of the valuable legislative history documents will be generated by the committee. The committee or subcommittee may hold hearings where interested members of the public and experts are invited to testify as to the potential impact of the bill. Transcripts of these committee and subcommittee hearings are generated at this stage of the legislative process.

C. Committee Report

When the committee has completed its consideration of the bill, it drafts a committee report explaining the bill and recommending whether the full chamber should pass the bill. The committee report often analyzes the bill section-by-section and thus is a very helpful document when researching legislative history. If the committee decides not to recommend passage, the bill dies in committee and usually no report is generated.

D. Reported Print

When a bill makes it out of committee, the committee report and a reported print of the bill are sent to the full chamber. A *reported print* is the version of the bill produced by the committee. The reported print may differ from the referred print (the version of the bill as it was originally sent to the committee). The comparison between these two documents can be valuable in gleaning legislative intent.

E. Full Chamber Consideration and Debate

Next, the full chamber considers the reported print of the bill. The transcripts of any floor debates that are part of this consideration may be reviewed when conducting legislative history research. Objections made and overcome by members of Congress may shed some light on the intent of the legislature when passing the bill.

F. Act Print

If the bill passes the originating chamber (either the House or the Senate), the act print of the bill is sent to the other chamber. The *act print* is the version of the bill passed by the first chamber. It is called an act print because once the bill has passed one chamber it is an "act." The whole process is repeated in the second chamber: referral to committee or subcommittee, reporting out of committee, debate, and voting. The act may die in the committee, may be passed by the chamber as originally worded, or may be passed with amendment or modification. If the language of the act passed in the second chamber has changed at all from the version that the first chamber passed, the act, as changed, must be sent back to the first chamber. If the amendments are controversial or substantial, a conference committee made up of members of both chambers may be convened to iron out details. Any conference committee report is a helpful legislative-history document. Ultimately, both chambers must pass identical bills, or the bill is defeated.

G. Enrolled Bill or Act

If both chambers pass an identical bill or act, the *enrolled bill*—the version of the bill passed by both chambers—is sent to the President to be signed. If the President signs the bill within ten days, it becomes law. If the President vetoes the bill, it goes back to Congress, and the veto may be overridden by a two-thirds vote of each chamber. If the President does not sign the bill within ten days, it automatically becomes law. However, if Congress adjourns during those ten days, the bill dies due to a "pocket veto."

H. Presidential Statement

The President may issue a statement upon the signing of a bill. Upon the veto of a bill, the President is required to indicate reasons or objections. Any presidential statement is clearly helpful in revealing executive intent, but it may also help reveal the intent of Congress. If, for example, the President makes certain objections in vetoing a bill and Congress then changes the bill to meet those objections, one may infer that Congress made changes to meet the President's objections.

V. Compiling Federal Legislative History

Each stage in the legislative process indicates a point where documents of recorded legislative history are created. As is true in any legal research, none of the documents uncovered can give you "the answer." Instead, the documents provide you with resources from which to make arguments about what Congress intended when it passed a certain statute.

A. Compiled Legislative Histories

As with other research, it is easier to find relevant information in a source with an indexing scheme. With legislative history research, often someone has not only created an index but also has compiled the legislative documents of the very statute in which you are interested. Always pursue the path of least resistance first.

A "compiled" legislative history "collects in one place either the texts of legislative documents pertaining to a statute or citations to the necessary legislative documents."[4] Legislative histories have been compiled for most major federal statutes. Compiled legislative histories should always be your first inquiry.

Three indexes of previously compiled legislative histories are available. A law library usually has at least one of these indexes in its collection. The first was compiled by Nancy Johnson and is entitled *Sources of Compiled Legislative Histories*. This index lists nearly all of the legislative histories that have been previously compiled. If you do not find a listing for a compiled legislative history of a statute in this index, one likely does not exist, and you must compile your own. Two other indexes of compiled legislative histories are *Union List of Legislative Histories*[5] and *Federal Legislative Histories: An Annotated Bibliography and Index to Officially Published Sources*.[6]

A researcher can search each index either by subject matter or by public law number. Recall from Chapter 2 that the public law number is listed immediately

---

4. Nancy P. Johnson, *Sources of Compiled Legislative Histories* i (2007).

5. Law Librarians' Society of D.C., *Union List of Legislative Histories* (2003).

6. Bernard D. Reams, *Federal Legislative Histories: An Annotated Bibliography and Index to Officially Published Sources* (1994).

after each statute in U.S.C., U.S.C.A., and U.S.C.S. Because many statutes have had several amendments and each amendment was in separate legislation, a researcher must look up each public law number in an index to locate all legislative history. Each index then refers you to the location of the actual legislative history. Be sure to check by subject matter and by public law number as each legislative history might not be found on both lists.

While all three indexes are published in books, the compiled legislative histories are usually available on microfiche. Working with the microfiche may seem tedious, but a compiled legislative history is the easiest way to gather the most comprehensive material available.

Compiled legislative histories will look totally different from each other and contain different information, even when they are compilations of the same act. Not all compiled legislative histories have the actual texts of debates and hearings. Some legislative histories are merely someone's interpretation of what the legislature thought and intended. Usually these interpretations include citations to the actual bills and reports to aid in research. The main advantage to these sources is that someone else has done most of the work, whether by compiling almost all of the actual documents in one place or digesting the main ideas from the actual documents.

Limited numbers of compiled legislative histories are available online. Lexis Advance organizes each compiled legislative history in a separate database, identified by the statute's popular name. These databases allow full-text searching. Some of the compiled legislative histories also include an index of the materials included. These indexes often include a list of documents that are available in the legislative history. Some indexes include section reference lists that enable a researcher to locate legislative history on a particular section of the legislation. WestlawNext maintains as part of its directory the Arnold & Porter Collection—Legislative Histories. Each actual compiled legislative history is its own database within that collection, and each database allows full-text searching.

Do not assume your work is completely done when you have found a compiled legislative history. Be sure to check for later amendments to your statute that were not included at the time the compiled legislative history was indexed. Legislative history documents on such amendments may be critical to interpreting the statute.

B. Compiling Your Own Legislative History in Print Sources

To compile your own legislative history, you must find and review the actual documents generated by Congress. Three print research sources are available to help you in this task. Two of these sources are *United States Code Congressional and Administrative News* (U.S.C.C.A.N) and *Congressional Information Service* (CIS). They will lead you to some of the same documents (e.g., Senate committee reports, House committee reports); however, CIS is more complete than U.S.C.C.A.N. because it points you to more legislative documents than U.S.C.C.A.N. does. The third source, *Congressional Record*, provides daily transcripts of Congressional floor debates.

1. *United States Code Congressional and Administrative News*

One source to consult when compiling a legislative history is *United States Code Congressional and Administrative News*. U.S.C.C.A.N. is published by West and contains both primary and secondary sources, including a reprint of the text of the federal statute and a very brief legislative history of the statute.

Each session of Congress will have multiple volumes of U.S.C.C.A.N. Each session is divided into two main sections, each of which may have more than one volume. One section is entitled "Laws" and is noted on the bottom black band on the spine. The second section indicates "Legislative History," "Proclamations," etc.

The "Laws" section of U.S.C.C.A.N. is a reprint of all of the statutes enacted by Congress during that session, arranged chronologically by public law and by *Statutes at Large* page numbers. Under the title of the act in the first volume will be a sentence that reads, "For Legislative History of Act, see p. ___." This sentence tells you exactly which page of the Legislative History volumes of U.S.C.C.A.N. to turn to for the legislative history of that act.

To use U.S.C.C.A.N. to find legislative history without first looking at the Laws section, start with the subject index located in the last volume of U.S.C.C.A.N. for that session of Congress. Because the volumes are not cumulative, you need to know either the session of Congress or the year in which the bill was passed to locate the correct volumes. Use descriptive words or the popular name of the act to search the subject index. The index will refer you to the page of the Legislative History section of U.S.C.C.A.N.

For example, in 2002, Congress enacted Anton's Law to improve child restraints in automobiles. Figure 7-2 illustrates the corresponding subject index listing in U.S.C.C.A.N. Under the heading "Children and Minors," and the subheading "Motor vehicles, restraints, improvements," the subject index provides both the *Statutes at Large* citation (116 Stat. 2772) and the applicable page of the Legislative History volume (page 1754).

Figure 7-2. *United States Code Congressional and Administrative News Subject Index — 107th Congress*

CHILDREN AND MINORS
Abuse, prevention month, proclamation, **A70**
Born Alive Infants Protection Act of 2002,
    116 Stat. 926, Leg. Hist. 620
Dot Kids Implementation and Efficiency Act
    of 2002, **116 Stat. 2766,**
    Leg. Hist. 1741
Health day, 2002, proclamation, **A164**
Immigration, **116 Stat. 927, Leg. Hist. 640**
Motor vehicles, restraints, improvements,
    116 Stat. 2772, Leg. Hist. 1754
National child's day, 2002, proclamation,
    A117
National domestic violence awareness month,
    2002, proclamation, **A161**
National mentoring month, proclamation, **A5**
National missing children's day, 2002, procla-
    mation, **A110**
Nutrition, **116 Stat. 134, Leg. Hist. 141**
Parents day, 2002, proclamation, **A129**

Source: United States Code Congressional and Administrative News, 107th Congress, Second Session, 2002, volume 4, at I6–I7 (2003). Reprinted with permission of Thomson Reuters.

You can bypass the subject index if you know the public law number or the *Statutes at Large* citation because the legislative histories of the public laws enacted by each Congress are arranged chronologically by public law number and *Statutes at Large* citation in U.S.C.C.A.N. Remember, the first number in the public law number citation is the number of the Congress enacting the law, and the second number is the consecutive number given to the act.

Figure 7-3 is an excerpt from the Legislative History entry for Anton's Law. In the Legislative History volumes, U.S.C.C.A.N. provides a listing of all congressional reports and the dates of consideration and passage of the bill in each house. The brief listing of legislative history provided there shows the path that a bill took to become Anton's Law, including the house of Congress in which the bill started. U.S.C.C.A.N. also provides the dates each house voted on the final bill and states which version of the bill was passed. U.S.C.C.A.N. cross-references the *Congressional Record* to lead you to the text of the floor debates in the House or the Senate.

This listing in the Legislative History volumes also indicates reports contained in U.S.C.C.A.N. In compiling U.S.C.C.A.N., the West publishers se-

Figure 7-3. *United States Code Congressional and Administrative News Legislative History—107th Congress*

ANTON'S LAW (IMPROVEMENT OF SAFETY OF CHILD RESTRAINTS IN PASSENGER MOTOR VEHICLES)

PUBLIC LAW 107–318, see page 116 Stat. 2772

DATES OF CONSIDERATION AND PASSAGE

House: November 15, 2002

Senate: November 18, 2002

Cong. Record Vol. 148 (2002)

**House Report (Energy and Commerce Committee)
No. 107–726, October 7, 2002
[To accompany H.R. 5504]**

The House Report is set out below.

HOUSE REPORT 107–726

[page 1]

The Committee on Energy and Commerce, to whom was referred the bill (H.R. 5504) to provide for the improvement of the safety of child restraints in passenger motor vehicles, and for other purposes, having considered the same, report favorably thereon with an amendment and recommend that the bill as amended do pass.

* * * * * * * * * *

Source: United States Code Congressional and Administrative News, 107th Congress, Second Session, 2002, volume 4, at 1754 (2003). Reprinted with permission of Thomson Reuters.

lectively choose the legislative history documents they believe are the most representative of the legislative intent behind each statute. For Anton's Law in Figure 7-3, the publishers chose House Report 107-726. While U.S.C.C.A.N. is not a comprehensive collection of all legislative history documents, it will usually have the originating committee's report and may have other important documents as well.

2. *Congressional Information Service*

The most complete source with which to compile your own legislative history is the *Congressional Information Service* (CIS). Since 1970, CIS has provided access to the hundreds of thousands of pages of documents created annually by legislative committees, subcommittees, hearings, debates, etc. Print volumes summarize and provide references to microfiche that contain the actual documents.

Each annual CIS collection since 1984 has had three types of volumes: index, legislative histories, and abstracts. Each annual set has a "User Guide" in each volume that explains how to use CIS and what kinds of things you can find in it. The "Index" volumes provide full access to all publications of Congress. These volumes are organized by subject matter, bill numbers, names of committee chairs, and names of witnesses. The "Legislative Histories" volumes of CIS compile the citations to all official publications, such as committee reports associated with each significant public law, except appropriations, passed by Congress. The "Abstracts" volumes provide a summary of each document to give the researcher sufficient detail to decide if a given document would be useful. Before 1984, CIS published only an index and an abstracts volume.

a. Index Volumes

All volumes of CIS are organized by year, including the Index volumes. The CIS Index is first issued monthly; each issue indexes the congressional publications of the prior month. The index is reissued in a quarterly publication and at the end of the year, resulting in an annual cumulative index contained in one hardbound volume. CIS also issues multiple-year indices that revise and cumulate all indexes for that time period.

These Index volumes actually contain several index listings. The "Index of Subjects and Names" is very extensive, including the names of witnesses. Each entry tells the subject of the document and the CIS accession number. The accession number is how CIS orders its Abstracts in the annual volumes and in the actual documents in the CIS microfiche collection.

The accession number contains both letters and numerals, such as S263-1. The letter before the numerals indicates the parent body (e.g., S for Senate), and the numbers identify the committee. CIS arranges legislative history document references according to the committees from which the documents originated. CIS has given each committee a code consisting of three numbers (e.g., 26 for the Committee on Commerce, Science and Transportation). The last number of the code identifies the type of document (e.g., 3 corresponds to a report). The last number after the hyphen represents the volume number of those documents in the microfiche (e.g., -1 is the first volume of the reports section). The Abstracts volumes—discussed below—contain a listing of these committee and document codes.

The CIS Index volumes contain two other helpful indexes in a "Supplementary Indexes" section, which follows the subject index. The "Index of Titles" is helpful when you know the title or popular name of an act. The "Index of

Bill Numbers" allows you to look up each version of a bill. This index may cover several congressional sessions; thus, you must be careful to look in the right part of the "Index of Bill Numbers."

b. Legislative Histories Volumes

In order to use CIS Legislative Histories volumes, you need to know (1) the public law number of the law or amendment and (2) the year of enactment. The "Table of Legislative Histories" tells you all the public laws for which there are legislative histories in the corresponding volume. Look under the "Public Law" heading to find information about the law or statute and where to find the text.

The next section of the CIS Legislative Histories volumes contains information on reports. All Senate and House reports generated on each bill are listed. Therefore, you need not worry about missing some pieces of information like you might with U.S.C.C.A.N. The short paragraph below the bold title is a brief description of the document. Figure 7-4 represents one of the committee report entries for Anton's Law in CIS.

To locate the complete text of this document, use the CIS accession number in the CIS microfiche collection. Some libraries do not contain CIS microfiche; instead, they maintain the Federal Depository Library collection microfiche. The government's SuDoc number is then used to access the Federal Depository Library collection microfiche. SuDoc stands for the "Superintendent of Documents." The SuDoc number usually begins with a letter, such as "Y" and includes the public law number. Every government document is assigned a number by the Superintendent of Documents.

Both the CIS accession number and the SuDoc number are located in italicized parentheses under the bold title of the report. In Figure 7-4, the CIS accession number is S263-1. The other reference is the SuDoc number (Y1.1/5:107-137). Use these numbers in the respective microfiche collections to locate the actual committee report.

The third section of any Legislative Histories volume is entitled "P.L. _____ Bills." This is an exhaustive listing of all the versions of bills introduced, when they were introduced, and which committee reported on each bill.

The fourth section is entitled "P.L. _____ Debate." Because debates occur on the floor of the Senate or House, they are part of the daily transcript printed in the *Congressional Record*, and cross-references to that resource are provided. No CIS or SuDoc numbers accompany the listed documents.

The fifth section of the legislative history is "P.L. _____ Hearings." The bold print sets out the title of the hearing, the body before whom the hearing

Figure 7-4. *Congressional Information Service Legislative History — Reports*

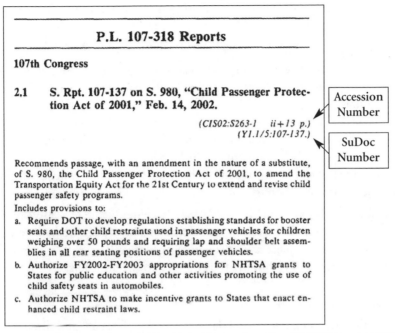

Source: *Congressional Information Service*, 2002 Legislative History, volume 33, at 431 (2002). Copyright 2002 ProQuest LLC. All rights reserved. Reprinted with permission.

took place, and the dates of the hearing. Below the CIS accession and SuDoc numbers is a brief summary of the subject matter of the hearing. Finally, under each hearing listing, a listing of witnesses' names appears, including their titles and who, if anyone, they represented.

The final sections are entitled "Committee Prints," "Documents," or "Miscellaneous." Not all sections appear with every act. These sections refer to any presidential remarks made upon signing the bill and other background research of the committee.

The legislative history section of CIS is very extensive, organized, and complete. Unfortunately, it is unavailable as a separate volume for laws enacted before 1984. From 1970–1984, the Index and Abstracts volumes of CIS provided the same information as in the current Legislative Histories volume—reports, bills, debates, and hearings—but not in as complete form.

The Legislative History volumes can help you identify potentially relevant documents. At this point, you should look at all of the abstracts of each document to which you have been referred to assess whether the document will be helpful.

c. Abstracts Volumes

The CIS Abstracts volume for each year is divided into three sections: House Committee publications, Joint Committee publications, and Senate Committee publications. Each section of the Abstracts volumes summarizes the main provisions of the committee reports. By looking at an abstract (see Figure 7-5), you can decide whether a document will help your legislative history research. If you decide that the document might be helpful, you would want to locate and read the full text of the document by using the CIS microfiche, the SuDoc microfiche, or the *Congressional Record*.

Abstracts volumes from 1970 to 1984 also contain the legislative histories information that is now in a separate volume. This legislative history section is not nearly as complete as the current Legislative Histories volumes but is definitely a short-cut to finding the citations to the abstracts.

3. Congressional Record

The *Congressional Record* is a daily transcript of debate and discussion on the floors of the House and the Senate. A separate paperbound volume is published for each day that Congress is in session and is also available online at www.congress.gov and www.gpo.gov/fdsys/. The *Congressional Record* contains various information including resolutions, debates, and copies of bills.

The *Congressional Record* is somewhat difficult to read because it is a chronological record of everything that happens on the floor of each house in the exact order in which it happened. Without some sort of index, you would have to skim through many pages of material to find the discussion relevant to the interpretation of the statute you wish to make. Fortunately, the *Congressional Record* provides two methods of searching the text. Approximately every two weeks, the *Congressional Record* publishes an index that indexes information by subject and Congress member's name. In addition, each individual volume of the *Congressional Record* has a Daily Digest summarizing major discussions it contains. The Daily Digest is divided into two sections: one for the Senate and one for the House. This digest tells you the page on which the subject matter in which you are interested is discussed.

Figure 7-5. *Congressional Information Service* Abstract

S263   Reports
COMMERCE,
SCIENCE, AND
TRANSPORTATION
Committee, Senate

S263–1   CHILD PASSENGER
          PROTECTION ACT OF 2001.
          Feb. 14, 2002.   107-2.
          ii+13 p.   S Doc Rm
          CIS/MF/3
          •Item 1008-C; 1008-D.
          S. Rpt. 107-137.
          °Y1.1/5:107-137.
          MC 2002-10093.

Recommends passage, with an amendment in the
nature of a substitute, of S. 980, the Child Passenger Protection Act of 2001, to amend the Transportation Equity Act for the 21st Century to
extend and revise child passenger safety programs.

Includes provisions to:

a. Require DOT to develop regulations establishing standards for booster seats and other
   child restraints used in passenger vehicles for
   children weighing over 50 pounds and requiring lap and shoulder belt assemblies in all rear
   seating positions of passenger vehicles.

b. Authorize FY2002-FY2003 appropriations
   for NHTSA grants to States for public education and other activities promoting the use of
   child safety seats in automobiles.

c. Authorize NHTSA to make incentive grants
   to States that enact enhanced child restraint
   laws.

S. 980 is related to H.R. 691.

In the *Congressional Record*, you can read the actual words spoken on the floor of the House and Senate during the debate of a bill. These comments

Figure 7-6. *Congressional Record* **107th Congress, November 14, 2002**

Mr. TAUZIN. Mr. Speaker, today we are considering an important and needed piece of safety legislation, H.R. 5504, the "Child Safety Enhancement Act of 2002." This bill, introduced by Rep. SHIMKUS, aims to protect the "forgotten child"—those children who are too large for the child safety seat, but too small for adult seat belts. Make no mistake about it, this bill will save the lives of innocent children who are too often the victims of automobile accidents.

This bill will enhance child passenger safety by requiring the National Highway Traffic Safety Administration (NHTSA) to draft a final rule establishing performance requirements for child restraints, including booster seats, for children weighing more than 50 pounds when riding in passenger vehicles, and the installation of three-point lap and shoulder belts in rear seats.

Source: 148 Cong. Rec. H8941 (daily ed. Nov. 14, 2002) (statement of Rep. Tauzin).

evidence at least what that member of Congress considered to be the legislature's intent. Figure 7-6 is the opening statement for Anton's Law. Without question, one concern of Congress was saving the lives of children who had outgrown car seats but did not yet fit regular seat belts. Be aware, though, that some material published in the *Congressional Record* in debate format may not have actually been spoken. Members of the House and Senate (and their staff) are able to submit written comments and revise spoken debate before publication.

C. Online Sources

Like online access to Missouri bills, electronic access to federal legislative history may also be more efficient than print sources. Also like Missouri sources, online federal resources are limited to legislation enacted relatively recently. Both Lexis Advance and WestlawNext only track bills back to 1991 and 1992.

1. Free-Access Sources

Two websites act as portals to government-sponsored websites that include legislative history documents. The Library of Congress maintains its website at http://www.congress.gov. It provides bill summaries and status, committee reports, and the *Congressional Record*. The Government Printing Office at www.gpo.gov/fdsys/ also contains the *Congressional Record* but adds bills and selected hearings and reports.

Both websites are efficiently used when you have a public law number or a *Statutes at Large* citation. Searching by descriptive words is available but may not be as efficient if the document does not contain those identical words.[7] Thus, you can best use these resources by locating the public law number first. Both in print and online in U.S.C., U.S.C.A., and U.S.C.S., the public law number follows the statutory language.

Another website that may be helpful in legislative history research is the National Archives website, which includes the Center for Legislative Archives, www.archives.gov/legislative/cla. That site provides links to finding aids for legislative records and congressional collections.

2. Fee-Based Sources

Both Lexis Advance and WestlawNext provide multiple databases to help researchers track pending and enacted legislation. Some are limited to specific topics, such as Lexis Advance's Bankruptcy Legislative Histories. Others are collections of several legislative histories, such as WestlawNext's Arnold & Porter Collection database. In addition, ProQuest Congressional is an electronic version of CIS. Like its print counterpart, ProQuest Congressional contains not only bills but also committee reports, committee hearings, and the *Congressional Record*.

D. Summary of Federal Legislative History Research

When determining federal legislative intent is important to analyzing a legal issue or advocating on behalf of a client, remember that the most efficient way to proceed is to locate a compiled legislative history. If none exists, you must compile your own using the sources that have been introduced in this chapter, including U.S.C.C.A.N., CIS, and the *Congressional Record*. Keep in mind that U.S.C.C.A.N. provides a pre-compiled legislative history by concentrating on the most important documents, while CIS provides the most complete index of abstracts to the actual documents of legislative history. The *Congressional Record*, on the other hand, is a transcript of Congressional floor debates.

---

7. This is a common problem with computer-assisted legal research, as explained in Chapter 8, and not unique to legislative history sources.

VI. Summary

The first step in analyzing any statute is to begin with its actual language. When a statute's language is ambiguous and a lawyer wants additional ammunition for a favorable interpretation, legislative history may provide insight into what the legislature intended the statute to accomplish. Thus, sound research skills in legislative history add to the lawyer's arsenal of available arguments.

Chapter 8

Online Research

I. Introduction

When used appropriatcly, computer-assisted legal research is of great benefit to the legal researcher. When used inappropriately, it drives up the cost of research for the client and wastes the attorney's valuable time. Computer-assisted legal research does not replace print research. There are times and places to use both.

Computer-assisted research is a part of an overall research plan. Thus, formulating a research plan includes determining which online resources to take advantage of and when to use them. Your goal should be cost-efficient, thorough research. As you become a more experienced legal researcher, you will be able to use the computer even more efficiently.

Continuing advances in technology will affect the resources that are available and how they can best be used. Because of these changes, any text focusing on the bells and whistles of any system will bc out-of-date before it appears in print. Thus, this chapter discusses the differences between free-access online sources and commercial online services. In addition, the chapter shows how to use the three approaches to legal research—known-authority, known-topic, and descriptive-word—with online sources. Lastly, this chapter provides general guidelines for choosing when to use print resources and when to use online services.

II. Not All Databases Are Alike

Beginning researchers often look at the computer as one large source of information. They choose a broad search engine, plug in a few words, and *voilà*, they get results. This process has worked well for them in researching topics from elementary school through some undergraduate courses. It does not work well in legal research for three reasons.

First, in law, it matters who provides the information. Are the words on a computer from the legislature, the highest court of the state, or a website entitled "Johnny's Ideas of What the Law Should Be"? Our system of jurisprudence is based on the concept of authority. The principle of *stare decisis* requires a later court to follow the decision of an earlier court with binding authority. Thus, the words found in a computer search must be words of authority that our system recognizes, and legal researchers must rely only on those computer databases that include that authority.

Second, a researcher must access the most current, up-to-date authority. Picture a computer as a room full of file cabinets. We have to pick the right file cabinet to locate what we need. We also need the most current files, not the outdated ones.

Third, legal research is most effective when it produces specific rather than general information. Information from Missouri is more relevant to a Missouri legal issue than information from Kansas. Continuing the file cabinet analogy, researchers try to refine searches to a more specific subset of the file cabinet — a drawer or a file folder depending upon how narrow the results should be.

A. Free-Access Online Sources

Some file cabinets, commonly referred to as databases, are accessible to all. These are typically government-sponsored websites or websites sponsored by academic institutions. No fee is charged to access any of the authority available.

Some of these sources are the print source in an online format. For example, judicial opinions are available on almost all court-sponsored websites. The printed slip opinion is made available as a PDF file or in another fashion. Advances in technology have enabled some websites to include search engines that allow a researcher not only to find documents more easily using a party's name but also to search the text of the document for specific language. Thus, a researcher can use keywords to find opinions and not have to know the date or a party's name.

These free-access websites have been referred to throughout this book for each type of authority. In addition, hyperlinks to various free-access sites are available through the "Research Bookmarks" link of the Leon E. Bloch Law Library of the University of Missouri-Kansas City School of Law's website at http://libguides.library.umkc.edu/content.php?pid=484186 or the "Online Resources" link of the University of Missouri Law Library at http://law.missouri.edu/library/resources. Members of The Missouri Bar can also link to these free-access sources through the bar's "Services and Resources" link at www.mobar.org. Click on "Practice Resources" and then "Online Resources" to get multiple links to Missouri's free-access sources.

Each free-access website is designed by the government or an academic sponsor. One uniform system or setup does not exist. As a result, how to use each website is individual to that website.

B. Commercial Online Services

Other file cabinets are accessible only by subscription. The most prevalent commercial providers are WestlawNext and Lexis Advance. Others include Bloomberg, VersusLaw and FindLaw.com. Fees are charged for a monthly subscription or an individual search. Fees are usually tailored to the different databases a law firm uses most frequently. For example, a Missouri law firm usually needs access to Missouri state law more than Alaska or Florida law. Thus, a Missouri firm will need access to a commercial database that includes Missouri cases, statutes, and regulations. A Missouri firm would rarely need access to a database with Alaska state regulations.

Each commercial provider has hundreds, if not thousands, of possible databases. A researcher could look at a database containing only Missouri state cases or a database that covers all fifty states' cases. Or, a researcher could look at only Missouri statutes or a database with all fifty states' statutes. Some databases are compiled by the level of court. One database provides all decisions of the United States Court of Appeals for the Eighth Circuit, and another database has those decisions plus the decisions of the district courts within that circuit. Still another database provides all decisions from all United States Courts of Appeals, and yet another provides all district court decisions. The choice of which database to choose is similar to deciding which digest to use. Start with the narrowest database and then branch out if your results are not what you need.

C. Missouri Bar Online Services

The Missouri Bar provides two noteworthy benefits in the area of online research. First is *The Missouri Bar Computer Network* (MoBar Net). Available since 1993, MoBar Net is a subscription-based service that provides limited legal resources. It includes local court rules, an index to Attorney General Opinions, and court information for both the Twenty-First and Twenty-Second Circuit Courts and the municipal courts in the St. Louis metropolitan area. The bulk of the site is devoted to factual records research, including Missouri

Driver's History and Dealer Information, criminal history record checks, and warrants in the St. Louis metropolitan area.

Second is Fastcase, a free service for Missouri Bar members, that provides basic online legal research capabilities at no cost. Members of The Missouri Bar have access to Missouri Supreme Court cases, Missouri Court of Appeals cases, RSMo, CSR, and Missouri Supreme Court Rules. In addition, Fastcase provides U.S. Supreme Court cases, U.S. Court of Appeals' cases, U.S.C., and CFR, as well as cases and statutes from all fifty states. All Missouri sources can be searched simultaneously. All cases can also be searched simultaneously. Missouri Bar CLE Deskbooks are included as an integrated part of the service.

For an additional charge, Missouri Bar members can subscribe to the Fastcase Premium Plan. The Premium Plan provides access to cases of the federal district courts, bankruptcy courts, and U.S. Customs Court, as well as Tax Court Memorandum Decisions and decisions of the Board of Tax Appeals.

III. Descriptive-Word Approach

Just as with print research, your work may require you to research issues with no known authority or topic. This section explains the process you should use in these situations. If you are new to online legal searches, your searches may be more successful if you complete the chart in Table 8-1 before beginning your search. Even after you become experienced in online searching, you should still keep notes containing the dates you searched, the searches you ran, and your results from the searches. These notes will help you stay on track while avoiding duplicating research later. Notes will also indicate the time period that needs to be updated as you near your project deadline.

A. Generate Descriptive Words

Begin a computer-assisted research project by making a list of descriptive words. Review Chapter 1 for suggestions on generating a comprehensive list of terms.

Using a print index allows you to quickly peruse other words that may not have occurred to you at first. The computer is not as forgiving, so remember to include on the list synonyms and related words. If you use only one word when a court could use several different words in its place and mean the same thing, then you may *never* find the cases that use words other than the one you entered. This is one reason to start in secondary sources and become fa-

Table 8-1. Example Notes for Online Searching

Date of Search: August 11, 2015

Issue: Whether a covenant not to compete is enforceable in Missouri

Online Site or Service: Lexis Advance

Filters: Missouri and Cases

Descriptive words: covenant, contract, non-competition, restraint of trade, compete, employee, employer, employment

Date Restriction: Last 10 years

Search: (covenant or contract) /p (non-competition or restraint of trade or compet!) /p employ!

Results: [You can list your results here, print a cite list to attach to your notes, or save the results to a Lexis Advance folder]

---

miliar with terms of art used in the area of law you are researching. WestlawNext does have a "Thesaurus" function and Lexis Advance has a "Suggest Terms" function. Both can assist you in generating more descriptive words.

Be sure to spell words correctly because the computer is literal. If you misspell a word, the computer does not correct it for you. Instead, the computer searches for the misspelled word. Unless the courts have misspelled the word in the same way, you will not find *any* authority. Lexis Advance now includes a "Check Spelling" function. Be sure to always proofread your search query; otherwise—garbage in, garbage out.

B. Choose an Online Service

Deciding which online source to use depends upon a variety of factors. One factor is your employer. Some law firms may have subscriptions to only one commercial provider. Another factor is the cost. The client you are working for may not pay or may limit what it will pay for commercial online research. The client matter may be too small in value to warrant more expensive computer-assisted legal research.[1] Still another factor is based upon personal preference. As you become a more accomplished legal researcher, you may prefer a specific service because of its features or its ease of use. Also consider the breadth of resources available through the service.

---

1. Some law offices negotiate a flat-rate subscription. The costs of individual searches is then not charged to particular clients in the same manner.

When possible, use free-access sources. The cost of commercial online services has been dramatically impacted by the availability and usability of free-access sources. Continued use of free-access sources should result in improved services and availability of the special features of commercial providers.

C. Choose a Database or Source

When researching primary authority in a commercial service such as Lexis Advance or WestlawNext, start in the database or source[2] that will give you mandatory authority for your issue. If you are not familiar with the databases available, both services have online directories. Clicking on the "i" next to the name of the database or source will provide information about its scope.

Try to restrict your search to the smallest set of sources or databases that will contain the documents you need. Because online databases correspond to many of the books you have used, it may be helpful to think of yourself in the stacks of the library when choosing sources or databases. Do you really want to search the contents of every reporter on the second floor, or do you want to search just *South Western Reporter* volumes for Missouri cases? In addition to producing a more focused set of results, smaller databases also tend to be less expensive than their larger counterparts.

D. Construct a Search

Both Lexis Advance and WestlawNext, as well as most search engines, allow you to conduct a search by simply typing in a single word. If the word is a term of art like "interpleader" or a cause of action that is less common, for example "kidnapping," this one-word search may be very successful. In contrast, if the search is for a broad area like "murder" or "jurisdiction," you will need to add more terms.

1. Boolean Connectors

More comprehensive searches usually result from the use of Boolean[3] connectors. These connectors tell the computer how the terms should be placed in relation to one another in targeted documents, enabling you to more accurately control what the computer searches to locate. To use Boolean connectors

---

2. Lexis Advance refers to its databases as "sources."

3. George Boole was a British mathematician. The Boolean connectors that carry his name dictate the logical relationship of search terms to each other.

Table 8-2. Boolean Connectors and Commands

Goal	Lexis Advance	WestlawNext
To find alternative terms anywhere in the document	or	or blank space
To find both terms anywhere in the document	and &	and &
To find both terms within a particular distance from each other	/p = in 1 paragraph /s = in 1 sentence /n = within a certain number of words	/p = in 1 paragraph /s = in 1 sentence /n = within a certain number of words
To find terms used as a phrase	leave a blank space between each word of the phrase	put the phrase in quotation marks
To control the hierarchy of searching	parentheses	parentheses
To exclude terms	and not	but not, %
To extend the end of the term	!	!
To hold the place of letters in a term	*	*

effectively, think of the ideal document you would like to find, and try to imagine where your search terms would be located in relationship to each other within that document. Would they be in the same sentence? The same paragraph? Table 8-2 summarizes the most common connectors and commands.

Terms and Connectors: Construct your computer search *before* you log on. Off-line, write out the query in plain English. Eliminate words that are too common to search. Consider synonyms for the remaining words. Then, list words in singular form, since programs automatically find plural forms. Choose endings and expanders. Choose connectors.

Using the example notes in Table 8-1, searching the terms *(covenant or contract) /p (non-competition or restraint of trade or compet!) /p employ!*, the computer will look for:

- Either the term *covenant* or *contract*

- Within the same paragraph as the term *non-competition* or *restraint of trade* or variations of *competition, compete, competitor*[4]

- and also in that paragraph variations of *employ, employee, employer, employment.*

Using Boolean connectors is essentially algebra with words.

Misuse of Boolean connectors can produce bizarre search results. If, instead of "/p" in the example above, the researcher used the "or" connector, the results could include a case in which high school students signed a *covenant* to remain celibate until marriage, a case concerning a *contract* for watermelons, and a case in which a golfer with a disability wanted to *compete* in a tournament without walking between holes.

Segment and Field Searching: Both Lexis Advance and WestlawNext allow you to search specific parts of documents, such as the date, the author, or the court. The options are available on drop-down menus. In Lexis Advance these specific parts are called document segments; in WestlawNext they are called fields. This type of search is added to the basic search with an appropriate connector.

Expanding or Restricting Your Search: Many of your initial searches will locate either no documents or more than 1,000 documents. Do not become frustrated. With practice, you will learn to craft more precise searches that produce more helpful results.

If a search produces no results, use broader connectors (e.g., search for terms in the same paragraph rather than in the same sentence), use more alternative terms, or use a larger set of sources or a larger database. If you still find nothing, consider reading a secondary source to increase your understanding of the issue, researching in print sources, or checking with your supervising attorney.

If your search produces a long list of results, skim them to see whether they are on point. If the results seem irrelevant, modify or edit your search query by omitting broad terms, using more restrictive connectors, or using a smaller set of sources or databases. You can also use the "Search Within Results" feature

---

4. The search engine will pull words that include a hyphen together with the same words without a hyphen.

on Lexis Advance or on WestlawNext to narrow your results further. These features allow you to construct a search within a search and produce a subset of the initial search results. These features may be cost efficient because they do not result in the additional charges of a new search.

2. Natural-Language Searching

Lexis Advance and WestlawNext allow natural-language searching, which may be most similar to the online searching you have done in the past. You simply type in a question or a list of words, and let the computer program decide which words are critical, whether the words should appear in some proximity to one another, and how often they appear in the document.

This type of search makes its "matches" based on the *location* or the *frequency* of the terms you requested. Location considers where your requested terms appear. The search engine assumes the best matches contain your words in the title, in a heading, or close to the beginning of the site. It may also consider how close together the requested terms are. Frequency-based searching evaluates how often your terms appear; in this case, the search engine assumes that a document that contains your terms more often will be more relevant.

Search engines using natural-language are designed to show you some results, even if the match does not seem very precise. Sometimes you will review the first ten matches, under the presumption that they are the best, and find that they are irrelevant to your search. This may mean that no better matches exist, that the search was not crafted well enough, or that this particular search engine did not scan the portion of the web that contains the needed documents. Be aware, too, that some matches appear first on certain search engines, not including Lexis Advance and WestlawNext, simply because sponsors pay for this privilege. Sometimes the best match from your perspective was the search engine's fourteenth best match, so skimming through the results is still very important.

While natural-language searching is unlikely to produce an exhaustive list of relevant authorities, it is likely to result in "one good case" that will spark other research through the known-authority approach. For this reason, some researchers like to conduct a natural language search early in their research. They skim through the search results quickly to see whether the search netted this one great catch. If so, they use its topics and key numbers or its core terms to find other cases, Shepardize or KeyCite it, and search article databases for articles that discuss it.

IV. When to Get Online

To ensure the most comprehensive, cost-effective results, use online and print tools in tandem. The following guidelines raise the issues you should consider in deciding where to look for the desired information—online or in print.

A. Scope of Source

Start with the tool that most specifically deals with the question. If you are not sure which tool does this, begin with print research. Use a print secondary source to increase your knowledge of the topic. Then, you can more accurately select a database. If there is a possibility that a state or the federal government could be involved in an area of regulatory law, begin with a free-access government website if the website has a search engine. If not, start in print sources to learn more about the topic.

Consider the subject, the type of authority available, and the coverage dates. As an example of a source that focuses on type of authority available, you have already seen in case law research that you should start with the narrowest digest available to you to locate relevant cases in a specific jurisdiction. A narrower digest gives you fewer extraneous cases.

As an example of time considerations, if you were looking for an opinion of the United States Supreme Court that was handed down yesterday, it would not yet be in print version waiting for you on the library shelf. In that instance, using online sources would be more effective.

After considering the subject, the type of authority available, and the coverage dates, use a source that provides comprehensive coverage. A looseleaf service in print or online may be the best option if the topic involves several different types of authority.

B. Overview

Select print sources when your purpose is to gain a general overview of the topic. Indexing and tables of contents of print resources make them easier to use if you are unfamiliar with the area of law. You can peruse these better than coming up with search queries in an unknown area.

C. Common, Ambiguous, or Broad Terms

Select print tools when your issue involves common or ambiguous terms. Commonly used words are unsearchable in an unstructured search in an online database. For example, the word "trust" occurs in estate planning and tax contexts as well as property law (deeds of trust) and remedies (constructive trusts). Procedural terms can be particularly frustrating to search online, as every case has some kind of procedural setting. Thus, an opinion might contain the words "summary judgment" but not focus on that civil procedure rule at all.

Also, begin with print tools when your problem concerns broad concepts such as due process, employment, or the Fourth Amendment. Use print sources to narrow your search to cases and statutes on point. Some broad concepts, however, have sufficiently unique terms or combinations that you can search online at an early stage by unique word patterns.

In contrast, go online to search unusual or unique words or distinctive terms of art. Online sources can readily assist you if you know the precise "phrase that pays" for your rule, such as "possession of burglar tools." A caveat—be sure you can reasonably rely on the use of the phrase. Could a judge write an opinion on this subject and not use the phrase? For example, a "covenant not to compete" looks unique but can also be called a non-compete clause or a noncompetition agreement.

D. Statutes

Use print sources first when attempting to locate statutes on a particular subject. Print indexes are quite specific and comprehensive. They are relatively easy to browse cost-effectively. But if you need to research several jurisdictions on the same issue, online research is more efficient.

V. Summary

Computer-assisted legal research is almost always a part of a research plan. Knowing when and how to use online sources is a valuable part of a researcher's repertoire of skills.

Do not be a slave to your computer. Be flexible; if computer research is not returning a quick answer to a research question, turn to print sources to increase your knowledge of the subject area. When you then return to computer-assisted legal research, you will be more efficient and better able to construct search queries focused on your issue.

Chapter 9

Research Strategies
and Organizing Research

I. Moving from Problems to Issues

Legal research begins with a problem. Clients do not come to an attorney with their legal issue well-formulated. They come with a problem they need to resolve. That problem can arise in many ways, and the following examples are merely representative. In private practice, a client comes for advice after being in a car accident. As in-house corporate counsel, an employer needs to revise employment policies. As a prosecutor, law enforcement has evidence of a crime. Each of these problems poses both fact issues and legal issues.

Fact issues and legal issues are not the same. A fact issue arises when there is a question about what actually happened. An example is whether a stoplight was red or green when a driver crossed an intersection. A fact issue is answered through evidence, such as witness statements. The judge or the jury, depending upon whether it is a bench trial or a jury trial, will decide what the fact was.

Before advising the client, an attorney needs to answer the legal issues raised by the facts. Solving legal problems requires knowing what law governs a set of facts. In most jurisdictions, a driver who crosses an intersection when a stoplight is red has violated one or more traffic laws. Discovering the laws that apply is the basis of analyzing legal issues and requires legal research.

Once an attorney knows what the facts are and what the law is, the attorney can analyze the situation and advise his client as to the best course of action. Should a dispute arise — the driver whose car collided with your client's car in the intersection has sued your client for damages — the judge will decide if your client's action violated the law. That is, the judge will apply the law to the facts.

Discovering what laws or rules apply to a legal issue is the heart of legal research. But legal research is not just collecting information. An attorney must objectively analyze issues in order to give sound advice. As a result, legal research is not a linear process. You do not start at point A, go through point B, and end at point C. Instead, as you find information, you analyze that information to better formulate your issue, which in turn highlights facts that are critical, which in turn narrows the scope of your issue, which in turn leads you to look for more specific authority, etc.

Understanding this non-linear nature of legal research should lead you to realize that you should use certain strategies to be sure you find the law or rules that apply to your specific legal issue. Applying the wrong rule can result in misinforming your client and violating the professional conduct code required of all attorneys; it can potentially lead to a malpractice action against you. To prevent that from occurring, be cognizant of the research process, plan your research, and organize your research results.

II. Understanding the Research Process

Legal research has one overarching goal — locating binding primary authority on point. Researchers can then use non-binding primary authority to illustrate or explain binding rules or argue for a change in the rule or a particular interpretation of a rule. Secondary authority is helpful in understanding the rule or the area of law to place the rule in context.

This book focuses on three approaches to legal research — descriptive-word, known-topic, and known-authority. In a research plan, a researcher uses all three approaches at some time. No set formula exists for where and how to begin. No researcher uses the exact same tools in the exact same order on every single issue she researches. Which approach to use and when to use it depends upon what the researcher already knows about the topic.

III. Planning the Research

This basic process must be customized for each research project. Consider whether you need to follow all eight steps in Table 9-1, and if so, in what order. If you are unfamiliar with an area of law, you should follow each step of the process in the order indicated. Beginning with secondary sources will provide both context for the issues you must research and citations to relevant primary authority. As you gain experience in researching legal questions, you may choose to modify the process. For example, if you know that a situation is controlled by a statute, you may choose to begin with that step. If you have known authority, you would begin with it. Choosing which of the eight steps to do online

Table 9-1. Overview of the Research Process

1. Determine which jurisdiction's *law applies.*

2. Generate a list of *descriptive words.*

3. Consult *secondary sources* and practice aids, including treatises, legal encyclopedias, and law review articles.

4. Find controlling *constitutional provisions, statutes,* or *regulations* by reviewing their indexes for your descriptive words, then reading the relevant sections.

5. Use *digests* or *online case-finding tools* to find citations to cases.

6. *Read* the cases.

7. *Update* your legal authorities to ensure they have not been repealed, reversed, modified, or otherwise changed.

8. *Outline* your legal analysis based on your research and *begin writing* your document.

---

is another part of the process. Using online resources are more appropriate for some steps than others and may be cost-prohibitive for some steps.

A. Determine What Law Applies

First, a researcher must know which jurisdiction's law controls the issue. Most of the time the answer is relatively straightforward. An accident occurs in a particular state. A contract states what law will apply. Sometimes, the issue is not so clear-cut. The area of conflicts of law provides rules to decide what law to apply. The researcher must then research the conflicts of law rule to determine what jurisdiction's law applies and then research that jurisdiction's law to see how it actually applies to the issue. In addition, a researcher must consider whether federal law, state law, or both apply.

Next, a researcher needs to know what is binding authority for that jurisdiction. Constitutional provisions, statutes, regulations, and judicial decisions of the highest court in that jurisdiction are all binding. As discussed in Chapter 1, intermediate appellate courts can also bind lower courts on some issues.

B. Generate Descriptive Words

Words are to an attorney what numbers are to a mathematician. They are our stock in trade. This book has focused on the necessity of beginning your research with a list of words geared to your issue. Chapter 1 suggests ways to think about issues to generate that list. A researcher uses words in a finding tool to locate helpful entries.

C. Consult Secondary Sources

Secondary sources are especially helpful when a researcher knows little to nothing about an area of law. Secondary sources help a researcher learn jargon and the "black-letter" law. Black-letter laws are the broad generalizations concerning an area of law that provide structure and reference for the topic. They provide context to see where a particular issue fits.

Secondary sources help a researcher know where to begin looking in primary authority. Besides understanding if the issue is governed by federal or state law, a researcher learns if the area of law includes constitutional provisions, statutes, or administrative regulations.

D. Find Constitutional Provisions, Statutes, or Regulations

Begin primary authority research by finding any constitutional provisions, statutes, or administrative regulations that apply to your issue. Starting with an annotated code also provides citations to judicial opinions and secondary sources.

While a researcher does not necessarily always start with these authorities, a researcher still includes this step to rule out these authorities. In Chapter 2, we saw that Missouri's constitution is quite statute-like and governs situations we would not ordinarily consider constitutional.

E. Use Digests or Online Case-Finding Tools

Take your list of descriptive words, and use print digests or online case-finding tools to locate judicial opinions on your issue. Some researchers prefer print digests as it is easy to scan several pages of headnotes rather than to look at them one-by-one on a screen. If the words are not getting results, go back to secondary sources to become more familiar with how words are used in that area of law. Some secondary sources will provide on-point topics and key numbers that you can take to digests. Remember that more than one topic and key number may apply to your issue.

F. Read Cases

Headnotes from digests are case-finding tools, not authority. Do not rely on the headnote. Locate the judicial opinion itself in the case reporter or online database. Read and analyze the opinion to determine whether it is on point with your issue.

G. Update Authority

Update, update, and then update again. Update specific authority as you determine it is on point. Update topics and key numbers to find additional authority. Update statutes and administrative regulations to find the most current version. At this point citators assist you in both verifying the law and in finding additional authority. Update authority later to see if there have been changes. Update one more time right before you submit your work to the court, to the partner, or to your client. Be sure you have analyzed the most current law that applies.

IV. Organizing the Research

Over time, researchers develop their own systems for organizing their research. Not having a system results in wasted time, missed resources, and missed authority. A research system should help you keep track of where you have already looked and what you have already found. Your system should be set up to avoid repeating steps and to help you use the information you find to solve the client's problem.

A. Keep Issues Separated

Most research problems will involve more than one legal issue. As a result, you should keep track of what you have found on each issue separately. An effective way to do that is to keep your research notes on each issue physically separated. Put your notes on separate legal pads, one for each issue. Keep separate folders or notebooks for notes and copies of authorities. Use dividers in a notebook to keep them separate. If you download copies of authority, keep them in separate folders on your computer. Use a spreadsheet to track the authorities for different issues. Both WestlawNext and Lexis Advance have folder systems to store your research. When you are unable to analyze the authority in full once you find it, using one of these features will prevent you from printing authority only to find it not helpful.

B. Keep Track of Where You Looked

As you conduct your research, keep track of where you search. This will keep you from losing focus as you do your initial research; it will also help you know how much updating you need to do at the end of your project.

Keep a running list of descriptive words you use to search indexes or to create online searches. As you think of more words, add them to your list. Keep track of which words you have used in each type of finding tool. Then as you get deeper into a research project and need to investigate new lines of analysis, you will remember where you have already been and which words you have actually used.

Maintain on a separate sheet of paper or in a separate computer file a list of finding tools you consult. List specific print sources (including the titles of secondary authorities, digests, and statutes) and online finding tools. For each source, note its coverage. List the main volumes and pocket parts of print sources separately, to be sure you have looked in both and to ease updating at the end of the project. For example, as you conduct your research, note "Missouri Digest 2d, Pocket Part ending with volume 195 S.W.3d," so you know that you have checked both the main volume and pocket part. Checking this list of finding tools at the end of the project, you will only have to see if a new pocket part has been issued without checking the entire pocket part. For each digest you use, note the topics and key numbers you have checked. Then, as you wind up your research, you will not have to check that digest again on the same topic and key number.

Keep track of specific online searches. Use Table 8-1 in Chapter 8 as an example. On your finding tools page, list the databases you have checked with the date, such as "Missouri Cases database on May 11, 2015." Then, to update you will only need to check opinions after that date. Likewise, use the History and Research Trail functions on WestlawNext and Lexis Advance to keep track of your online searches and their results.

C. Keep Track of What You Looked At

In addition to a finding tools page, keep a separate page that lists what you have found. Table 9-2 illustrates one format to use. A full citation is not needed here; just a list of partial cites is fine. Listing sources on a spreadsheet will allow you to reorder the authorities by volume number for easy check of new authorities. When you find a new case or statute, check this list first to be sure you have not already looked at that authority.

Table 9-2. Taking Notes on Authority

Authority	On Point or Helpful?	Table of Authorities (TOA) Check	Citators Check
§ 569.180 RSMo	✓	N/A	5/11/15
686 S.W.2d 19	✓	5/9/15	5/9/15 5/25/15
452 P.2d 832	No	—	—

D. Keep Notes on the Authority Itself

Keep your notes on each authority on a separate page. Include the information you need to properly analyze the authority and to be able to write from your notes easily. For a case brief, no formal organization is required, but include the following:

- Citation — Put the authority in correct citation format from the beginning. This will keep you from having to go back to the original source to track down missing information.

- Facts — Focus on the legally determinative facts, those that made a difference in the outcome. Keep this section fairly brief unless the facts are similar to yours in several ways.

- Holding and reasoning — Summarize the court's analysis. Address only the parts of the opinion that address your issue. If you jot down any of the exact language of the opinion, note that with quotation marks.

- Pinpoint pages — Keep track of the page numbers of the court's analysis to make your citation easier when you write. Be especially careful with online versions of cases as a change in page is indicated by an asterisk or two, and the opinion will include pagination that reflects multiple print reporters, if available.

- Headnote numbers — Make note of particularly relevant headnote numbers to use with citators. Remember that West headnotes are used in KeyCite and LexisNexis headnotes are used in Shepard's.

- Reflections — Include your own thoughts about the opinion. What questions are left unanswered? How do you plan to use this opinion in your analysis?

- Citators — Print the citing list from your citators check to keep with your notes of this case. Keep track of any negative treatment of your case. Remember that negative treatment may concern a different issue addressed in the opinion. Note any negative treatment either directly on the list of citing sources or in your notes. Also note any relevant prior or subsequent history of the case.

E. Don't Be a Slave to the Printer or Copy Machine

One mistake new legal researchers often make is to print or make a copy of every single case they are referred to in their research. They end up with a two-foot high stack of paper, most of which is irrelevant. Resist the temptation to print. Read the case in the reporter or online first to be sure it is truly relevant and that you will actually use it later.

V. Knowing When to Stop

One of the problems with the circular nature of legal research is knowing when to stop. No clear end point exists. New judicial opinions are printed daily, and the possibility always exists that new authority will be published on your issue. Some guidelines may help you decide when to stop.

A. Hit Paydirt

If you find the answer, your research is complete. If you are still uncertain of the answer, you are not done.

B. Found Relevant Authority

Even without finding a clear answer, you can stop researching when you have found relevant, recent authority. For example, you have found several controlling authorities that agree as to the rule on the issue. They are recent enough — within the past ten to fifteen years — and you have run your citators check so that you are comfortable the rule has not been changed.[1] Secondary sources and persuasive authorities from other jurisdictions agree with your finding of the rule. Contrary authorities can be distinguished on the facts.

---

1. Even older cases can still be good law. In some areas of law, such as property, change occurs relatively slowly. That case on donative intent for a gift from 1930 may still be a correct statement of the rule.

C. Looked Every Important Place

If you do not find relevant authority, your research may still be complete if you have searched thoroughly. For example, you have checked secondary sources, cases, statutes, administrative regulations, and the constitution. You have checked several other jurisdictions to see their rules on the issue. You have exhausted your synonyms of words and are confident you have been thorough. The reality may well be that there is no authority on your exact issue. At that point, consider analogous rules that could be extended to your facts. Then begin another research project on those rules.

D. Cost Exceeds Benefit

Not every research project requires the same exhaustive research approach. The research you do for a scholarly law review article will be extensive and cover every single possibility. Sometimes, however, you need a quick answer to a legal problem, and there is simply no time to be exhaustive. Other times the client's resources and the firm's resources do not support exhaustive research.

A practicing attorney's cost reflects both time and money. With experience doing research, you will become more efficient, and you will be able to do exhaustive research in much less time.

E. Achieved Closure

Stop researching when further research turns up nothing new and you are referred back to authorities you have already found. Updating every authority reveals no new authority. You are truly going in circles. Then, you can stop.

VI. Preparing to Write — Outline Analysis

Placing this step last may imply that analysis is done at the end of research. But analysis is on-going. Researchers analyze issues as they research.

Outline the rule into its elements or factors. Include key statutory language. Jot down potential fact comparisons between the facts of the problem and the facts of cases. Consider counter-analysis your opponent will raise. Analysis must be objective — weighing the strengths and weaknesses of every position. Only through this careful look at both sides of an issue can you give sound advice. This preliminary outline will point out holes in your research that you need to fill.

Table 9-3. Elements Chart

Element	Rule	Fact Comparison	Fact Application	Conclusion
1.				
2.				
3.				
Exceptions?				
4.				

If outlining is too restrictive, consider using a chart to organize all the elements or factors of a rule, similar to Table 9-3, following the typical legal analysis formula of Issue-Rule-Application-Conclusion (IRAC). As you conduct your research, your chart will become more sophisticated and detailed. You may find that you need to rearrange your chart to better fit the elements or factors.

An outline or chart is one of the best ways to visualize the big picture of your analysis and to see its various components. The outline or chart should enable you to synthesize the law, apply the law to your client's facts, and reach a conclusion on the desired outcome. Applying the law to your client's facts may lead you to research issues that may not be apparent in a merely theoretical discussion of the law.

In the "rule" section, be sure to keep the focus on the language of your rule. In the rule column, quote the rule as it is stated in the statute and in judicial opinions. Indicate what authority gives you that part of the rule by placing the code section or the case name with the page number where the rule is found in parentheses right after the rule. Focusing on the language of the rule makes it easier to synthesize the rule in your writing. If you focus on each authority, you will be tempted to write about each authority separately. This kind of authority-by-authority writing is not really analysis but a book report or summary of each authority.

The "application" part of IRAC has two parts: fact comparison and fact application. Fact comparison is showing how your client's facts are like or unlike the critical facts of a case. Fact application is applying the client's facts to the rule. These are not necessarily separated in legal writing. Indeed, most good legal writers weave their fact comparisons into their fact application as a seamless analysis.

VII. Summary

The goal of any legal research problem is to find a solution to the client's problem. Sometimes, the answer is not what the client wants. Instead of just telling the partner there is no way to achieve the client's desired goal, be creative and think of possible solutions.

Appendix A

Legal Citation[*]

I. Introduction

To convince another lawyer or a judge that you thoroughly researched your argument and that your ideas are well-supported, you must provide references to the authorities you used to develop your analysis and reach your conclusion. These references are called *legal citations*. They tell the reader where to find the authorities you rely on and indicate the level of analytical support those authorities provide.[1] In a legal document, every legal rule and every explanation of the law must be cited.

Legal citations are included in the text of legal documents rather than being saved for a bibliography.[2] While you may initially feel that citations clutter your document, you will soon learn to appreciate the valuable information that they provide.

The format used to convey that information, however, requires meticulous attention to such riveting details as whether a space is needed between two abbreviations. In this respect, citation format rules can be like fundamental writing rules, which are based on convention, not reason. Why capitalize the personal pronoun "I" but not "we" or "you" or "they"? Why does a comma signify a pause, while a period indicates a stop? Rather than trying to understand why citations are formatted the way they are, the most practical approach is simply to learn citation rules and apply them. Frequent repetition will make them second nature.

---

[*] Portions of this chapter were drawn from *Oregon Legal Research* by Suzanne E. Rowe.

1. ALWD & Coleen M. Barger, *ALWD Guide to Legal Citation* (5th ed. 2014) (*ALWD Guide*).

2. Some attorneys place citations in footnotes. Before doing so, be sure to check any local court rules and any guidelines of your employer.

Table A-1. Purposes of Legal Citations

- Show the reader where to find the cited material in the original case, statute, rule, article, or other authority.

- Indicate the weight and persuasiveness of each authority, for example, by specifying the court that decided the case, the author of a document, and the publication date of the authority.

- Convey the type and degree of support the authority offers, for example, by indicating whether the authority supports your point directly or only implicitly.

- Demonstrate that the analysis in your document is the result of careful research.

Source: ALWD Guide.

Of the many different citation systems that exist, this chapter addresses the two national citation manuals, the *ALWD Guide to Legal Citation*[3] and *The Bluebook: A Uniform System of Citation.*[4] In law practice, you may encounter state statutes, court rules, and style manuals that dictate the form of citation used before the courts of different states. You may find that each firm or agency that you work for has its own preference for citation or makes minor variations to generally accepted format. Some law offices have their own style manuals, drawn from state rules and national manuals. Once you learn what your employer's preferences are, adjust your citation format to that style. In law school, learn the style of the teacher for whom you are working or the journal of which you are a member. Once you are aware of the basic function and format of citation, adapting to a slightly different set of rules will not be difficult.

II. National Citation Manuals

Student editors of four Ivy League law reviews developed citation rules that are published as *The Bluebook: A Uniform System of Citation*, now in its twentieth edition. For many years, the *Bluebook* was the only national citation system that was widely recognized. Many law firms, agencies, and organizations still consider *Bluebook* citations the norm, although few practicing lawyers know its current rules; most assume that the *Bluebook* rules have not changed since they were in law school.

---

3. ALWD & Coleen M. Barger, *supra* note 1.
4. *The Bluebook: A Uniform System of Citation* (The Columbia Law Review et al. eds., 20th ed. 2015) (*Bluebook*).

For practicing attorneys, the primary difficulty with the *Bluebook* is that it includes *two* citation systems: one for law review articles and another for legal memoranda and court documents. Most of the *Bluebook*'s over 500 pages are devoted to citations used for articles published in law journals. The rules most important to attorneys—those concerning legal memoranda and court documents—are given relatively scant attention in the *Bluebook*.

Legal writing faculty nationwide sought to resolve this problem. The *ALWD Guide* takes the *Bluebook*'s two systems and puts them together to be less confusing. The explanations are clear, and the examples are useful to both law students and practicing attorneys. As a result, learning citation from the *ALWD Guide* is generally not as confusing as learning from the *Bluebook*. The citations using the *ALWD Guide* and the citations created from the *Bluebook* are identical.

This section explains how to use both the *Bluebook* and the *ALWD Guide* in writing memoranda and briefs. In addition, Section III explains local rules. Section IV explains how to use the *Bluebook* and the *ALWD Guide* in writing articles for scholarly publication. An author submitting an article for publication in a law review that adheres to *Bluebook* rules should follow *Bluebook* citation format, available in both the *Bluebook* and the *ALWD Guide*.

A. Organization and Finding Tools

1. Bluebook

a. Reference Guide and Bluepages

Perhaps the most helpful information in the *Bluebook* is the reference guide on the inside back cover of the book, which gives examples of citations used in court documents and legal memoranda.[5] At the beginning of each rule, an example is given in larger type with blue dots to indicate appropriate spacing. Another helpful portion of the *Bluebook* appears near the beginning—the Bluepages. They provide information for and additional examples of citations used in documents other than law review articles. This section illustrates items that should be italicized or underlined in citations in legal memoranda and court documents. These include case names, titles of books and articles, and introductory signals. Everything else appears in regular type. Remember to follow these instructions even when the *Bluebook* examples include large and small capital letters.[6]

---

5. Examples of law review citations are found on the inside front cover.

6. The *Bluebook* permits the large and small capital letters typeface for court doc-

b. Index

The index at the back of the *Bluebook* is quite extensive, and in most instances it is more helpful than the table of contents. Most often, you should begin working with the *Bluebook* by referring to the index. Index entries given in black type refer to citation instructions, while index entries in blue refer to examples. Remember that the examples in the body of the *Bluebook* are in law review style. If you are writing a document other than a law review article, you will need to refer also to the Bluepages at the front of the book and the examples inside the back cover to see how you must modify the examples.

2. *ALWD Guide*

Because the *ALWD Guide* combines the *Bluebook*'s two systems of citation for law reviews, memoranda, and briefs, its organization is much more straightforward. All examples show the proper typeface and include a small green triangle to indicate spaces between abbreviations.

Each rule begins with a "Fast Formats" section to illustrate the rule. A list of "Fast Formats" appears on the inside front cover. Next, "Snapshots" are annotated reproductions of print sources to highlight features. Frequent charts and generous use of white space lead to an easier read. A detailed index is followed by a brief chart for finding short citation formats for commonly used sources. Law review format is shown at the end of each rule.

B. Citing Missouri Material

Because the *ALWD Guide* and the *Bluebook* are designed for national use, they have abbreviations for some Missouri material that differ from what Missouri practitioners and Missouri courts use. The most obvious difference is that *Revised Statutes of Missouri* is abbreviated "Mo. Rev. Stat." instead of "RSMo." Since an attorney working in Pennsylvania would not be expected to know whether RSMo refers to the statutes of Missouri or Montana, the additional information given by the longer abbreviation is necessary. Thus, a full citation to a Missouri statute would be Mo. Rev. Stat. § 569.120 (2000). In addition to using a different abbreviation, Missouri practitioners and courts also reverse the order of the citation and place the section number prior to the abbreviation: § 569.160 RSMo 2000.[7]

---

uments and memoranda for stylistic reasons. All examples in the Bluepages follow the traditional and commonly used approach of employing roman and italics typeface only.

7. Some practitioners place the date in parentheses as the national citation manuals do.

Missouri practitioners and courts also always include a designation of which intermediate appellate court division has issued an opinion. This designation is prohibited by the *Bluebook*. The *ALWD Guide* suggests using the designation if highly relevant.

A summary of abbreviations for Missouri material appears in both the *Bluebook* and the *ALWD Guide*.

C. Incorporating Citations into a Document

You must provide a citation for each idea that comes from a case, statute, article, or other source. Thus, paragraphs that state legal rules and explain the law should contain many citations.

A citation may offer support for an entire sentence or for an idea expressed in part of a sentence. If the citation supports the entire sentence, it is placed in a separate *citation sentence* that begins with a capital letter and ends with a period. If the citation supports only a portion of the sentence, it is included immediately

Table A-2. Examples of Citation Sentences and Citation Clauses

Citation Sentences: First-degree burglary involves a building or an inhabitable structure. § 569.160 RSMo 2000. The term inhabitable structure is defined as "a ship, trailer, sleeping car, airplane, or other vehicle or structure where any person lives or carries on business." § 569.010(2)(a) RSMo 2000.

Citation Clauses: Missouri statutes define both first-degree burglary, § 569.160 RSMo 2000, and second-degree burglary, § 569.170 RSMo 2000.

Do not cite your client's facts or your conclusions about a case, statute, or other authority. The following sentence should not be cited: "Under the facts presented, our client's conduct would fall under first-degree burglary, since a homeless family sometimes slept in the building he broke into." These facts and conclusions are unique to your situation and would not be found anywhere in the reference source.

D. Case Citations

A full citation to a case includes (1) the name of the case, (2) the volume and reporter in which the case is published, (3) the first page of the case, (4) the exact page in the case that contains the idea you are citing (i.e., the *pinpoint* or *jump* cite), (5) the court that decided the case, and (6) the date the case was decided. The key points for citation to cases are given below, along with examples.

1. Essential Components of Case Citations

Include the name of just the first party on each side, even if several are listed in the case caption. If the party is an individual, include only the party's last name. If the party is a business or organization, shorten the party's name by using the abbreviations in the *ALWD Guide* or in the *Bluebook*. Table A-3 illustrates a sample of abbreviations.

Table A-3. Word Abbreviations in *ALWD Guide* and *Bluebook*

Associate	Assoc.
Association	Ass'n
Center	Ctr.
Commissioner	Comm'r
Department	Dep't
University	Univ.

Between the parties' names, place a lower case "v" followed by a period. Do not use a capital "V" or the abbreviation "vs." Place a comma after the second party's name.

The parties' names may be italicized or underlined in memoranda and briefs.[8] Use the style preferred by your supervisor, and use that style consistently throughout each document. Do not combine italics and underlining in one cite or within a single document.

EXAMPLE: *Union Elec. Co. v. Mo. Dep't of Conserv.*, 366 F.3d 655, 658 (8th Cir. 2004).

Next, give the volume and the reporter in which the case is found. Pay special attention to whether the reporter is in its first, second, or third series. Abbreviations for common reporters are found in both the *ALWD Guide* and the *Bluebook*. In the example above, 366 is the volume number and F.3d is the reporter abbreviation for *Federal Reporter, Third Series*.

---

8. Law review articles use a different typeface explained *infra* at IV.

After the reporter name, include both the first page of the case and the pinpoint page containing the idea that you are referencing, separated by a comma and a space. The first page of the above case is 655, and the page where your idea came from is 658. If the pinpoint page you are citing is also the first page of the case, then the same page number will appear twice even though this seems repetitive.[9]

In a parenthetical following this information, indicate the court that decided the case, using abbreviations in the *ALWD Guide* and in Table T1 of the *Bluebook*. The abbreviations for the courts of each state are included in parentheses just after the name of the court. In the above example, the Eighth Circuit Court of Appeals, a federal court, decided the case.

If the reporter abbreviation clearly indicates which court decided a case, do not repeat this information in the parenthetical. To give two examples, only cases of the United States Supreme Court are reported in *United States Reports*, abbreviated U.S. Only cases decided by the Illinois Appellate Court are reported in *Illinois Appellate Court Reports*, abbreviated Ill. App. Repeating court abbreviations in citations to those reporters would be duplicative. By contrast *South Western Reporter, Third Series*, abbreviated S.W.3d, publishes decisions from different courts within several states; so, the court that decided a particular case needs to be indicated parenthetically. Thus, in the last example below, "Ark." indicates that the decision came from the Arkansas Supreme Court rather than from another court whose decisions are also published in this reporter.

EXAMPLES: *Brown v. Bd. of Educ.,* 349 U.S. 294, 300 (1955).
Rosier v. Cascade Mt., Inc., 367 Ill. App. 3d 559, 562 (2006).
Davis v. Parham, 208 S.W.3d 162, 162 (Ark. 2005).

Note that these court abbreviations are not the same as postal codes. Abbreviating the Arkansas Supreme Court as either AR or Arkan. would be incorrect.

The final piece of required information in most cites is the date the case was decided. For cases published in reporters, give only the year of decision, not the month or date. Do not confuse the date of decision with the date on

---

9. When using an online version of a case, remember that a reference to a specific reporter page may change in the middle of a computer screen or a printed page. This means that the page number indicated at the top of the screen or printed page may not be the page where the relevant information is located. For example, if the notation *658 appeared in the text before the relevant information, the pinpoint cite would be to page 658, not page 657.

which the case was argued or submitted, the date on which a motion for re-hearing was denied, or the publication date of the reporter.

2. Full and Short Citations to Cases

The first time you mention a case by name, you must immediately give its full citation, including all of the information outlined above. Even though it is technically correct to include the full citation at the beginning of a sentence, a full citation takes up considerable space. By the time your reader gets through the citation and to your idea at the end of the sentence, the reader may have lost interest. Table A-4 demonstrates this problem.

Table A-4. Examples of Full Citations

Assume that this is the first time the case has been mentioned in this document.

CORRECT:	Legislative intent is first determined by examining the statute. *Tilley v. State*, 202 S.W.3d 726, 736 (Mo. Ct. App. 2006).
CORRECT: (but should be avoided)	In *Tilley v. State*, 202 S.W.3d 726, 736 (Mo. Ct. App. 2006), the court noted that legislative intent is first determined by examining the statute.

After a full citation has been used once to introduce an authority, short citations are subsequently used to cite to this same authority. A short citation provides just enough information to allow the reader to locate the longer citation and find the pinpoint page.

When the immediately preceding cite is to the same source and the same page, use *id.* as the short cite. When the second cite is to a different page within the same source, follow the *id.* with "at" and the new pinpoint page number. Capitalize *id.* when it begins a citation sentence, just as the beginning of any sentence is capitalized.

If the cite is from a source that is not the immediately preceding cite, give the name of one of the parties (generally the first party named in the full cite), the volume, the reporter, and the pinpoint page following "at."

EXAMPLE: Open and notorious possession requires the claimants
to prove that the owners had notice the claimants were

asserting title to the disputed property. *Williams v. Frymire*, 186 S.W.3d 912, 920 (Mo. Ct. App. 2006). Visible acts of ownership amount to sufficient notice. *Id.* Construction of a fence is recognized as an example of open and notorious possession. *Flowers v. Roberts*, 979 S.W.2d 465, 471 (Mo. Ct. App. 1998). Improvements to the property are not required. *Williams*, 186 S.W.3d at 920–21. Minimal and sporadic possessory acts, however, are not sufficient to constitute open and notorious possession. *Flowers*, 979 S.W.2d at 470–71.

If you refer to the case by name in the sentence, your short citation does not need to repeat the case name. The last sentence of the example would also be correct as follows: "In *Flowers*, minimal and sporadic possessory acts were not sufficient to constitute open and notorious possession. 979 S.W.2d at 470–71."

The format consisting of just a case name and page number, *Flowers* at 471, is incorrect. The volume and reporter abbreviation are also needed.

3. Prior and Subsequent History

Sometimes your citation needs to show what happened to your case at an earlier or later stage of litigation. The case you are citing may have reversed an earlier case, as in the example below. If you are citing a case for a court's analysis of one issue and a later court reversed only on the second issue, you need to alert your reader to that reversal. Or, if you decide for historical purposes to include in your document discussion of a case that was later overruled, your reader needs to know that as soon as you introduce the case. Prior and subsequent history can be appended to the full citations discussed above.

EXAMPLE: The only time that the Supreme Court addressed the requirement of motive for an EMTALA claim, the court rejected that requirement. *Roberts v. Galen of Va.*, 525 U.S. 249, 253 (1999), *rev'g* 111 F.3d 405 (6th Cir. 1997).

E. Federal Statutes

The general rule for citing federal laws is to cite the *United States Code* (U.S.C.), which is the official code for federal statutes. In reality, that publication is published so slowly that the current language will most likely be found in a commercial code, either *United States Code Annotated* (published by West) or *United States Code Service* (currently published by LexisNexis). A cite to a

Table A-5. Common Signals

No signal	• The source cited provides direct support for the idea in the sentence. • The cite identifies the source of a quotation.
See	• The source cited offers implicit support for the idea in the sentence. • The source cited offers support in dicta.
See also	• The source cited provides additional support for the idea in the sentence. • The support offered by *see also* is not as strong or direct as authorities preceded by no signal or by the signal *see*.
E.g.	• Many authorities state the idea in the sentence, and you are citing only one as an example; this signal allows you to cite just one source while letting the reader know that many other sources say the same thing.

federal statute includes the title, code name, section, publisher (except for U.S.C.), and date. The date given in statutory cites is the date of the volume in which the statute is published, not the date the statute was enacted. If the language of a portion of the statute is reprinted in the pocket part, include the dates of both the bound volume and the pocket part. If the language appears only in the pocket part, include only the date of the pocket part.

> EXAMPLE: (Statutory language appears in both the bound volume and the supplement):
> 18 U.S.C.A. § 4247 (West 2012 & Supp. 2015).
> EXAMPLE: (Statutory language appears in just the supplement):
> 18 U.S.C.A. § 4247(a)(1)(c) (West Supp. 2015).

F. Signals

A citation must show the reader that you understand the level of support each authority provides. You do this by deciding whether to use an introductory signal and, if so, which one. The more common signals are explained in Table A-5.

G. Explanatory Parentheticals

At the end of a cite, you can append additional information about the authority in parentheses. Sometimes this parenthetical information conveys to the reader the weight of the authority. For example, a case may have been decided *en banc* or *per curiam*. Or the case may have been decided by a narrow split among the judges who heard the case. Parenthetical information also allows you to name the judges who joined in a dissenting, concurring, or plurality opinion.

An explanatory parenthetical following a signal can convey helpful, additional information in a compressed space. When using this type of parenthetical, be sure that you do not inadvertently hide a critical part of the court's analysis at the end of a long citation, where a reader is likely to skip over it.

> EXAMPLE: Excluding relevant evidence during a sentencing hearing may deny the criminal defendant due process. *Green v. Georgia*, 442 U.S. 95, 97 (1979) (per curiam) (regarding testimony of co-defendant's confession in rape and murder case).

H. Quotations

Quotations should be used only when the reader needs to see the text exactly as it appears in the original authority. Of all the audiences you write for, trial courts will probably be most receptive to longer quotations. For example, quoting the controlling statutory language can be extremely helpful. As another example, if a well-known case explains an analytical point in a particularly insightful way, a quotation may be warranted.

Excessive quotation has two drawbacks. First, quotations interrupt the flow of your writing when the style of the quoted language differs from your own. Second, excessive use of quotations may suggest to the reader that you do not fully comprehend the material; it is much easier to cut and paste together a document from pieces of various cases than to synthesize and explain a rule of law. Quotations should not be used simply because you cannot think of another way to express an idea.

When a quotation is needed, the words, punctuation, and capitalization within the quotation marks must appear *exactly* as they are in the original. Treat a quotation as a photocopy of the original text. Any alterations or omissions must be indicated. Include commas and periods inside quotation marks; place other punctuation outside the quotation marks unless it is included in the original text. Also, try to provide smooth transitions between your text and the quoted text.

I. Noteworthy Details

Paying attention to the following details will enhance your reputation as a careful and conscientious lawyer.

- Use proper ordinal abbreviations. The most confusing are 2d for "Second" and 3d for "Third" because they differ from the standard format.

- Do not insert a space between abbreviations of single capital letters. For example, there is no space in U.S. Ordinal numbers like 1st, 2d, and 3d are considered single capital letters for purposes of this rule. Thus, there is no space in P.2d or F.3d because 2d and 3d are considered single capital letters. Leave one space between elements of an abbreviation that are not single capital letters. For example, F. Supp. 2d has a space on each side of "Supp." It would be incorrect to write F.Supp.2d.

- In citation sentences, abbreviate case names, court names, months, and reporter names. Do not abbreviate these words when they are part of textual sentences; instead, spell them out as in the example below.

EXAMPLE: The Ninth Circuit held that Oregon's Measure 11 did not violate constitutional rights provided under the Eighth and Fourteenth Amendments. *Alvarado v. Hill*, 252 F.3d 1066, 1069–70 (9th Cir. 2001).

- It is most common in legal documents to spell out numbers zero through ninety-nine and to use numerals for larger numbers. However, you should always spell out a number that is the first word of a sentence.

J. Differences in Lay-out Between *ALWD Guide* and *Bluebook*

The only differences between the *ALWD Guide* and *Bluebook* are the rule numbers and the lay-out of the text in each book. You will never need the rule numbers in practice. Some law review editors request a student staff member to include the rule number when they are correcting changes in the citations. The authors of the *ALWD Guide* have conversion charts for your quick reference to each rule number. You can locate these charts on the Association of Legal Writing Directors' website, www.alwd.org/publications/citation-manual/. You do not need to purchase both books.

In the *ALWD Guide*, the academic format is shown at the end of each rule. This style is designated by a notation of "Academic Footnote" in a small bar on the right together with a red line on the left margin. After the rule number is the additional symbol (FN). For example, the rule for typeface for case names in case citation is found in Rule 12.2(a)(2)(FN). Thus, a student or lawyer need look in only one place to see examples for law review citations and for memoranda and briefs.

In the *Bluebook*, the examples in the main part of the text are in law review style. The student or attorney must refer back to the Bluepages to understand format for memoranda and briefs.

Both the *Bluebook* and the *ALWD Guide* use the exact same format for all citations. Both use a different typeface for legal memoranda and for law review citations.[10]

III. State Citation Rules

Most states have their own rules of citation, called *local rules*. Missouri does not. These local rules differ somewhat from the rules in the two national citation manuals. If you work in another state, follow that state's local rules or use the format given in the *ALWD Guide* or the *Bluebook*, depending on your supervisor's preferences. In the state of Illinois, for example, the Illinois Supreme Court requires citation to include the official reports citation, *Illinois Reports* or *Illinois Appellate Court Reports*.[11]

IV. Citations for Law Review Articles

Using the *Bluebook* to write citations for law review articles is considerably easier than using it for practice documents. As noted above, almost all of the examples given in the *Bluebook* are in law review format.

Law review articles place citations in footnotes or endnotes, instead of placing citations in the main text of the document. Most law review footnotes include text in ordinary type, in italics, and in large and small capital letters. This convention is not universal, and each law review selects the typefaces it will use. Some law reviews may use only ordinary type and italics. Others may use just ordinary type.

---

10. *Infra* part IV.
11. Ill. Sup. Ct. R. 6.

Table A-6. Comparison of Formats

Legal Memoranda	Law Review Articles
Kan. Stat. Ann.	KAN. STAT. ANN.
§ 59-2233 (2005).	§ 59-2233 (2005).

The typeface used for a case name depends on (1) whether the case appears in the main text of the article or in a footnote and (2) how the case is used. When a case name appears in the main text of the article or in a textual sentence of a footnote, it is italicized. By contrast, if a footnote contains an embedded

Table A-7. Typeface for Law Review Footnotes

Item	Type used	Example
Cases	Use ordinary type for case names in full citations. (See text for further explanation.)	Legal Servs. Corp. v. Velazquez, 531 U.S. 533 (2001).
Books	Use large and small capital letters for the author and the title.	DAVID S. ROMANTZ & KATHLEEN ELLIOTT VINSON, LEGAL ANALYSIS: THE FUNDAMENTAL SKILL (2d ed. 2009).
Periodical Articles	Use ordinary type for the author's name, italics for the title, and large and small capitals for the periodical.	Colin B. Picker, *Neither Here Nor There — Countries That Are Neither Developing Nor Developed in the WTO: Geographic Differentiation As Applied to Russia and the WTO*, 36 GEO. WASH. INT'L L. REV. 147 (2004).
Explanatory Phrases	Use italics for all explanatory phrases, such as *aff'g, cert. denied, rev'd*, and *overruled by.*	Legal Servs. Corp. v. Velazquez, 531 U.S. 533 (2001), *aff'g* 164 F.3d 757 (2d Cir. 1999).
Introductory Signals	Use italics for all introductory signals, such as *see* and *e.g.* when they appear in citations, as opposed to text.	*See id.*

citation, the case name is written in ordinary text. Similarly, when a full cite is given in a footnote, the case name is written in ordinary type. But when a short cite is used in footnotes, the case name is italicized. Assuming you are submitting an article to a law review that uses all three typefaces, dictate which typeface to use for each type of authority. Tables A-6 and A-7 illustrate the use of these typefaces.

Law review footnotes generally use short cites the same as in other documents. The short cite *id.* can be used only if the preceding footnote contains only one authority. One unique requirement is the "rule of five." This rule states that a short cite *id.* can be used if the source is "*readily found in one of the preceding five footnotes.*"

V. Summary

To be sure that the citations in your document correctly reflect your research and support your analysis, you should include enough time in the writing and editing process to check citation accuracy. As you are writing the document, refer frequently to the local rules or the citation guide required by your supervisor. After you have completely finished writing the text of the document, check the citations carefully again. Be sure that each citation is still accurate after all the writing revisions you have made. For example, moving a sentence might require you to change an *id.* to another form of short cite, or vice versa. In fact, some careful writers do not insert *id.* citations until they are completely finished writing and revising.

Sometimes editing for citations can take as long as editing for writing mechanics. The time invested in citations is well spent if it enables the person reading your document to quickly find the authorities you cite and to understand your analysis.

Appendix B

Selected Bibliography

General Research

Steven M. Barkan et al., *Fundamentals of Legal Research* (10th ed. 2015).
Robert C. Berring & Elizabeth A. Edinger, *Finding the Law* (12th ed. 2008).
Morris L. Cohen & Kent C. Olson, *Legal Research in a Nutshell* (11th ed. 2013).
Christina L. Kunz et al., *The Process of Legal Research, Authorities and Options* (8th ed. 2012).
Amy E. Sloan, *Basic Legal Research: Tools and Strategies* (5th ed. 2012).
Christopher G. Wren & Jill Robinson Wren, *The Legal Research Manual: A Game Plan for Legal Research and Analysis* (2d ed. 1986).

Specialized Research

Kenneth Culp Davis, *Administrative Law Treatise* (3d ed. 1995).
Joan S. Howland & Kay M. Todd, *Principles of Power Research* (West 1993).
Nancy P. Johnson, *Sources of Compiled Legislative Histories: A Bibliography of Government Documents, Periodical Articles, and Books* (2007).
Law Librarians' Society of D.C., *Union List of Legislative Histories* (7th ed. 2003).
Office of the Federal Register, *The United States Government Manual* (Nat'l Archives & Records Administration 2013).
Bernard D. Reams, *Federal Legislative Histories: An Annotated Bibliography and Index to Officially Published Sources* (1994).

Legal Analysis

John Dernbach et al., *A Practical Guide to Legal Writing & Legal Method* (5th ed. 2013).
Richard F. Neumann, Jr., *Legal Reasoning and Legal Writing: Structure, Strategy, and Style* (7th ed. 2013).
Richard F. Neumann, Jr. et al., *Legal Writing* (3d ed. 2015).

Laurel Currie Oates & Anne Enquist, *The Legal Writing Handbook: Analysis, Research, and Writing* (6th ed. 2014).

Mary Barnard Ray & Barbara J. Cox, *Beyond the Basics: A Text for Advanced Legal Writing* (2d ed. 2003).

Index